The New Con Synthesizer

A Comprehensive Guide to the world of Electronic Music by **David Crombie.**

THE ART DIRECTOR WOULD LIKE TO THANK DAVE CAULFIELD AT 'AKAI',
JERRY UWINS AT 'YAMAHA', NICK HARRIS AND THE STAFF AT 'CHROMATIX'
FOR THEIR HELP WITH THE COVER.

Omnibus Press
London/New York/Sydney/Cologne

INTRODUCTION

The aim of this book is to provide the reader with a reference work that will help him or her to understand the increasingly complex world of electronic music synthesis. This book caters for both the person with little or no knowledge of synthesizers, and for those with a working understanding of these electronic instruments.

Technology has "gone mad" over the past few years, and as a result we have now entered a new generation of such instruments. Hence we have decided to give this book the title "The New Complete Synthesizer" to mark this technological transition.

This book starts with the basics, which are fairly easy to get to grips with, and on these foundations a complete understanding of the subject can be built. The information is such that the impatient novice can glean a certain amount by skip reading through the book, but those with some knowledge will find a vast amount of new material to get your teeth into, including developments such as FM Synthesis, and the so-far extremely confused subject of MIDI.

THE NEW SYNTHESIZER

In 1982 I wrote a book entitled "The Complete Synthesizer", and the original intention was to update that work to incorporate the various new developments. It soon became apparent that this was not a satisfactory solution. A fresh approach was called for as a response to the dramatic changes that have recently taken place in electronic instrument technology. And to really identify these revolutions it was decided to call this publication "The New Complete Synthesizer".

You may have a copy of "The Complete Synthesizer", and unfortunately, of necessity there will be some overlap in the two books. But I hope that you will appreciate the need for the inclusion of some of the more fundamental sections, and still find value in the considerable amount of new material.

CONTENTS

Author: Dave Crombie
Art Editors: Nick Harris,
David Whelan

Art Director: Mike Bell

Typeset by: Capital Typesetters,
28 Poland St.
London W1.

Printed in England by:
Ebenezer Baylis & Son Limited
The Trinity Press, Worcester,
and London

Music Sales Corporation
24 East 22nd Street, New York,
NY 10010, USA

Exclusive distributors:
Book Sales Limited
78 Newman Street,
London W1P 3LA, England

The publishers
27 Clarendon Street, Artarmon,
Sydney, NSW 2064,
Australia

This book © copyright 1986 by
Omnibus Press
(A division of Book Sales Limited)
78 Newman Street,
London W1P 3LA, England

ISBN 0.7119.0701.3
UK Order No. 43421

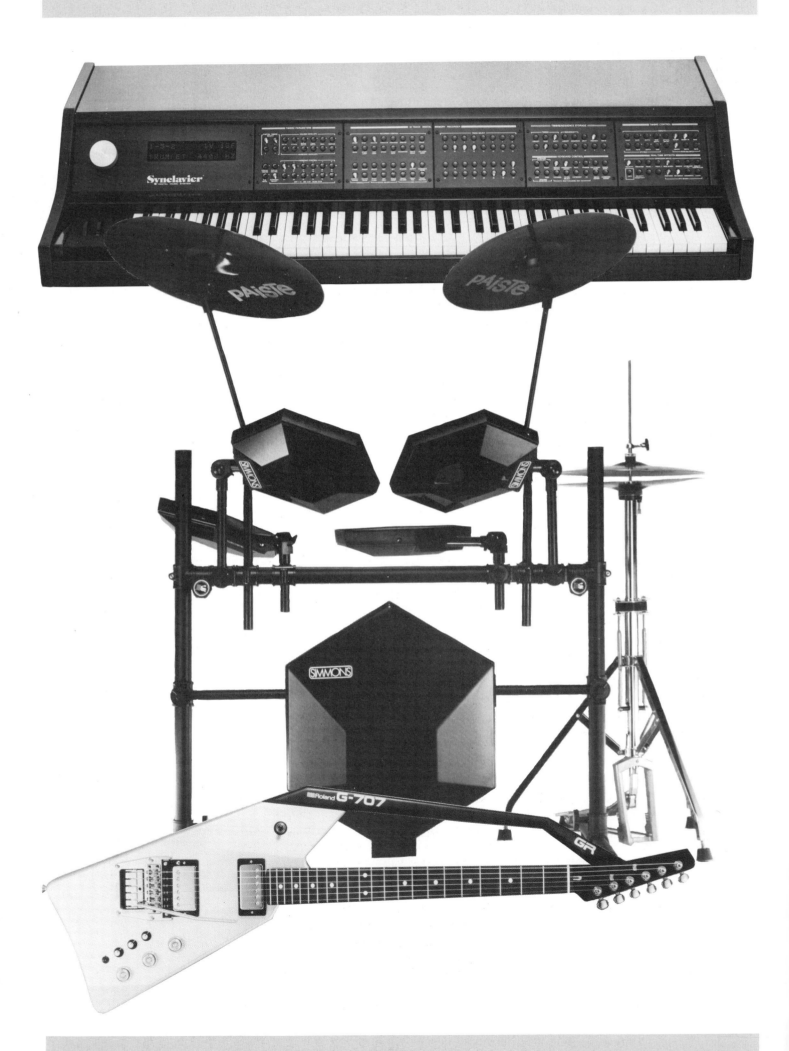

PREFACE

Synthesis is the process of combining basic fundamental elements to create a whole new entity, i.e. to make a complex item from a set of simple ones.

The term crops up in all walks of life. The one we all know best from schoolday biology is probably that of photo-synthesis, where light is used by plants to construct complex substances from simple mediums such as carbon dioxide and water.

Electronic sound synthesis is a similar concept, in that a complex noise or sound can be "constructed" by defining simple fundamental elements. Think of any sound, say someone hitting a glass bottle with a spoon. What is it that makes that sound unique? What is it about the sound that enables us to perceive what we are hearing, even if we cannot physically see it?

Every sound is made up of three basic elements: pitch, tone, and volume. By determining the "value" of these three parameters we can create a specific sound. An electronic sound synthesizer is a device that does just that.

If we take things a stage further and add some form of control element – for example a chromatic keyboard – we have a more useful device, the electronic music synthesizer. The remainder of this book attempts to explain everything you ever needed to know about it.

To the uninitiated the synthesizer appears as a complex mass of knobs and switches, and even in these more technologically minded times, many people are put off by the very term synthesizer. An electronic piano is obviously a device with a keyboard that makes piano sounds, and somehow derives its sound electronically. A synthesizer is a somewhat less tangible object.

"I know it makes all kinds of weird and wonderful 'Star Trek' type sounds, but what exactly is it for?" Many people look on the synthesizer as a professional's musical instrument, the kind of thing that just rock and pop people use, but things are changing.

Around the turn of the century, most well-to-do homes had an acoustic piano. The home organ took over in the 50s and 60s. Today smaller portable home keyboards offering preset sounds with automatic rhythms and chordal accompaniments are becoming increasingly popular. But more and more people want to be able to create their own sounds, and not just to rely on sounds set into the instrument at the factory.

Creativity, suprisingly enough, is the key word, and like the great painters you can only be truly creative by starting from scratch, mixing your own colours and constructing a masterpiece that is totally your own. Painting by numbers with coloured paints supplied has only a limited fascination, and little satisfaction. The electronic music synthesizer is the first truly creative musical instrument . . . and anyone can use it.

Whither Technology and Music?

Robert Moog, the man credited with making the synthesizer commercially and artistically acceptable, once said that musical instrumentation reflects the technology of the day. Consider a violin; isn't that a bizarre piece of musical hardware? A strangely shaped hollow wooden box, with 'f' shaped holes, and a long flat protrusion over which pieces of cat gut are held in tension . . . etc. etc. The violin reflected the wood crafting skills of the era, as did the pianoforte. Today we are in an electronic age, and it is only natural that we should employ today's technology to produce a new quality of music. The synthesizer was possible thanks only to the electronic revolutions of the 50s and early 60s. Today the instruments have become more advanced with the evolution of the microprocessor.

Is a synthesizer a synthesizer?

Going into a music store and asking for a synthesizer is like going into your local library and asking for some books. There are many different kinds of synthesizer, all designed to fulfil a different role. For example, a musician using a synthesizer live on stage will require a different kind of instrument from someone who wants to use a synthesizer to supplement the sounds of his electronic organ at home; and the person working with the synthesizer in a recording studio will also have his own specific requirements.

Some synthesizers are designed for solo/lead line work, while others are used simply as a backing simulating string-like sounds.

And of course a synthesizer doesn't have to be controlled from a keyboard. There are guitar synthesizers, wind synthesizers, percussion synthesizers, computer controlled and so on.

Hopefully, by the time you finish this book, you will have a clear idea of the role of the synthesizer, and why it is such an important musical development.

Why do most synthesizers have keyboards?

The keyboard has certainly come to be the most widely used way of controlling a synthesizer for three prime reasons:

1 Since the keyboard is, in essence, just a row of peculiarly shaped switches, it is particularly suitable for interfacing with the electronic circuitry of the synthesizer.

2 The keyboard is certainly the most efficient device with which to feed information from man to machine. The ten digits of the human hands can be used to provide up to ten separate sets of note information, i.e. what notes are to sound and when. With a guitar you can at best pluck only five notes at once (five fingers); if you're clever you can play four notes at once on a xylophone (using four beaters), while all wind instruments can produce only one note at a time.

3 The first synthesizers used keyboards as the controllers.

Imitative or abstract synthesis?

A synthesizer can be used in two ways:

1 To copy an existing sound. It can be used to produce the sound of a violin, a French horn, an electronic organ or even a lawnmower, but when used for this purpose we are dealing with imitative synthesis.

2 To create an entirely new sound, i.e. one that we wouldn't hear from another source. For example, you may be familiar with the type of sound that was very popular in the early days of the synthesizer. This is abstract, or imaginative, synthesis.

Allied to imitative synthesis is sampling. Sampling involves manipulating a real sound to produce the desired aural effect. Strictly speaking sampling is not a form of synthesis as we are, effectively, starting with the end product. Nevertheless this is an increasingly important subject in the field of new synthesis, and we shall be dealing with this technology in detail.

What use is a synthesizer?

It is all very well stating that a synthesizer can create all manner of amazing sounds, and copy existing ones by the process of specifying the values of a host of basic ingredients, but of what use is such a machine?

In simplistic terms, there are six main tasks for which the synthesizer is used:

1 In a band (rock, jazz, folk etc,) to provide extra tone colours, or a symphonic backdrop: imitative and/or abstract. Synthesizers can even be used to replace all conventional electric and/ or acoustic instruments in a band.

2 As an "add-on" to the home/cabaret/theatre organist providing extra tone colours: primarily imitative.

3 As a source instrument for a home recording facility: imitative and/or abstract.

4 As a jack-of-all trades instrument in the professional recording studio: imitative and/or abstract.

5 As a sound effects generator for use on film and television soundtracks, (sometimes even for home movies): imitative and/or abstract.

6 As a home computer peripheral: imitative and/or abstract.

There are other uses to which the synthesizer can be put, e.g. as a piece of test equipment for testing loudspeakers, amplifiers, microphones, etc. But here we have the six main roles of the synthesizer. All six areas will be fully dealt with in this book.

SOUND & ELECTRICITY 1

The end product of working with an electronic synthesizer is sound. We are striving to create specified sounds that our ears can detect and consequently our brains can perceive.

As stated in the Preface, synthesis is the art of creating sounds from basic building blocks. Consequently, in order to be able to create a certain sound from scratch, it is necessary to know exactly what sound is, and how it behaves. Most of today's synthesizers are designed so that you can just switch on the instrument and select pre-programmed sounds at the touch of a button. But when it comes to creating your own voicings you need to be aware of certain fundamental pieces of information. We shall be devoting the majority of this chapter to the physics of sound.

Music synthesis involves the processing of "electricity". And there are close ties between the subjects of sound and electricity, so we shall be concentrating also on relevant electronic principles in this chapter. Don't worry, it's not as difficult as it appears.

What is Sound?

Sound is the sensation we experience when movement or vibrations in the air are detected by our ears. Our ears convert these vibrations into minute electrical pulses that are transmitted *via* our nervous system to the brain.

The air around us is made up of billion upon billion of microscopic particles. You cannot see them, because they are so small, but they are there. These particles make up the atmosphere of our planet. And it is these air particles that transmit the sound from its source to our ear.

How? By moving backwards and forwards to form denser and less dense variations in the air.

Take as an example a loudspeaker from a hi-fi system. Remove the front of the speaker cabinet, and put on a heavy rock record (if you possess such a thing), and look closely at the cone of the large speaker. You'll see that it is moving to and fro very quickly, and usually you'll notice that it responds most dramatically every time the bass drum is played.

Consider what happens when we send a constant low pitched tone to the loudspeakers. If the pitch is low enough, again we shall see the cone vibrating. But what is happening with respect to the air particles?

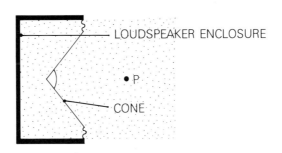

1 When there is no sound emanating from the loudspeaker the air particles surrounding the unit are pretty well randomly distributed.

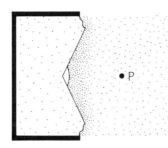

2 As the tone is introduced, the speaker shoots forward compressing the particles immediately surrounding the cone.

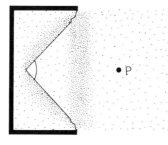

3 Having reached its maximum projection, the speaker then retreats from its initial position causing the air particles to become less densely packed (known as rarefaction), but to establish this rarefaction particles further removed from the speaker have in turn to be compressed.

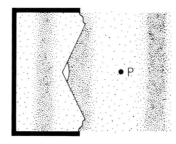

4 The process continues to repeat itself until the situation shown in 5 exists.

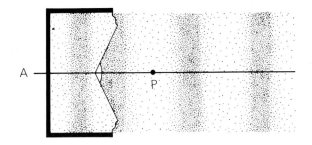

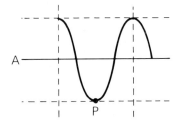

5 Here we have a train of compressions and expansions emanating from the loudspeaker. If we were to consider an imaginary line drawn along the axis AA of the loudspeaker, at a given instant in time we can see how the speaker has caused the density of the air particles to vary.

The ear detects changes in air pressure and it is these changes we perceive as sound. Our ears act as the loudspeaker did, but in reverse. The changes in the air pressure cause a membrane within the inner ear to move back and forth, sending a nervous signal to the brain.

The above example of the loudspeaker is somewhat simplified. In reality the changes in air density caused by our rock music recording would be far more complex.

It should be noted that it is not the particles that move from the source to the listener. It is the variation in the air particle density that changes. This is illustrated by checking the movements of point 'P' (which represent a specific air particle) on the diagrams.

It is the air particles that transmit sounds from source to receiver.

I'm sure you are familiar with the schoolday experiment that proves the above statement, of placing a ringing alarm clock in a bell jar and pumping out the air to leave a virtual vacuum. As the air is removed the sound becomes weaker and weaker, until it is almost inaudible. As soon as air is restored to the jar, it is possible to hear the ringing again. This proves that it is air particles that transmit sonic information.

The Three Elements of Sound

When we hear a sound, it can be defined at any one instant by considering three different parameters: the pitch, the timbre (from the French word for tone colour), and loudness or amplitude.

Unfortunately, it's not that simple. You might be listening to an orchestra, where the sound from many sources combines. Here it would be necessary to make a composite analysis.

It should also be stressed that these three parameters continually change throughout a note. Consider the following figure. Here we are examining a period of, say, ten seconds. After one second a single note on a piano is played, and the changes in pitch, timbre and amplitude detailed.

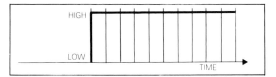

PITCH: As you can see (and hear) the pitch remains pretty well constant – unless we have a particularly poor quality piano.

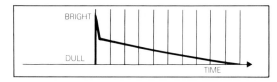

TIMBRE: The tone starts off being fairly bright, caused by the piano's hammer striking the strings, and becomes more mellow as the note dies away.

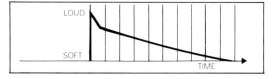

AMPLITUDE: The amplitude is nil before a note is played; it then shoots up to a maximum value as the note is played, and gradually decreases as the note fades away.

We can create virtually any sound at every given instant in time if we can specify its pitch, timbre and amplitude. This sounds as if it is a long and laborious process, and so it would be if we had to break the sound down into fractions of a second and specify each parameter. As we shall find, however, the design of most synthesizers is such that we are concerned with shapes. These can be used to provide the changes in the sound quickly and efficiently.

Let's now look more closely at these three elements . . .

Waveforms

With figure 6 we have introduced the concept of the waveform. This idea of the waveform is most important in the understanding of many elements of synthesis.

The graphical representation of how the density of the air particles varies with distance from the tuning fork gives rise to the smoothly undulating shape depicted. As the tuning fork is oscillating back and forth, it constantly retraces the same curve.

Some of you may remember another schoolroom experiment where a small pen-like device is fitted to the end of a tuning fork, and a sheet of paper, attached to a board, is suspended in such a way that as the fork vibrates it traces a wavy line on the passing paper.

As the paper moves at a constant speed you would find that a repeating waveform such as that shown would result.

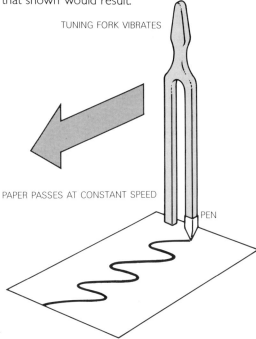

TUNING FORK VIBRATES

PAPER PASSES AT CONSTANT SPEED

PEN

If with this experiment we were to theoretically 'halt' the paper, i.e. change the terms of reference, we would find that the sound waves are moving away from the source at a specific rate (in this case the speed of sound). We could also consider any static position and look at the variation in air density caused by the sound, every hundredth of a second (say). Because of the fixed speed of the sound waves, this would produce an identically shaped plot.

Waveforms are generally represented as variations of some parameter with respect to time. The horizontal axis is used to read off the time, and the vertical axis is the value of the parameter in question.

Different shaped waveforms do not have the same tonal quality, but if they oscillate at the same frequencies they will produce a similar pitch.

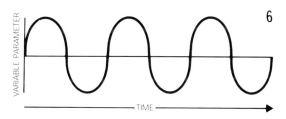

6

VARIABLE PARAMETER

TIME

Frequency, Pitch, and Music

The human ear can generally detect frequencies between 20 cycles per second and 20,000 (20k) cycles per second. This corresponds to wavelengths between 16.5m, and around 1-1/2 cms.

The important thing to remember is that frequency is an exact measurement, but pitch relies on mathematical relationships between the frequencies of notes. If you don't understand that – read on.

Every note we hear or play has, by definition, a basic pitch, i.e. it oscillates so many times per second. But in order to make musical sense of frequencies we have to introduce the concept of the octave, and this is the most important single thing on which our whole understanding of Western music is based.

Hum a note. Now raise the pitch of the note you are humming, but remember your original note. You will find that in the course of your humming, you will reach a note that sounds similar to the one you started with. Hum the two of them alternately. It feels as if there is a close similarity between them, but you can definitely tell that they are pitched differently. One sounds 'higher' than the other.

You are in fact humming two notes that are an octave apart. And were you to examine their waveforms you would see that they had the same basic shape, but that the higher note repeated its cycle at twice the rate of the lower (see figure 7). This span between notes, known as the octave, sounds 'right' to the Western ear. The octave acts as the basis for all our music, so it makes sense to split the entire range of audible frequencies into octaves.

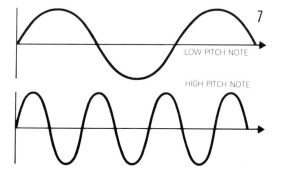

7

LOW PITCH NOTE

HIGH PITCH NOTE

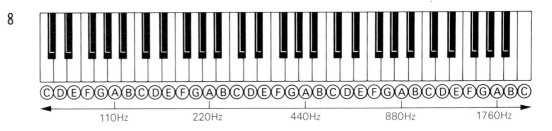

8

Figure 8 shows graphically, part of the span of the audio spectrum. This ranges from 20 to 20,000 cycles per second. At this stage, (for the sake of argument) let's take a point of reference somewhere around 440 cycles per second. The reasons for this will soon become clear. A note an octave above it will oscillate at twice the frequency (880 Hz), while a note an octave below will oscillate at 220. By doubling and halving frequencies, we can divide the audio frequency into five octaves as shown.

Don't try to hum five different notes which sound the same, the range of the human voice isn't as good as that of the human ear. You should at best be able to reach four similar sounding notes, then you can say your voice has a three octave range.

When we use musical instruments we obviously don't just use frequencies that are simple multiples of themselves; we split the octave into 12 smaller divisions. And each of these is a note with a name. Originally the octave was split into seven, and each of the notes was given a letter to identify it – A, B, C, D, E, F, and G.

Again hum a note and then hum the note you think to be the next comfortable one above it. Repeat the exercise for another note, and at each stage think of that note as being identified by the next letter in the alphabet. You should find that by the time you get to G the next note sounds exactly an octave above the first.

It is important to realise that frequency and pitch do not have a simple relationship to one another. Look at the figure again. The note an octave below the 440 cycle mid-point oscillates at 220 cycles, i.e. that octave spans 220 cycles (440-220), but the span of the octave above the 440 Hz mid-point spans 440 cycles (880-440). So you can see that an octave doesn't equate to a fixed number of cycles. Remember, doubling the frequency raises the pitch by one octave.

Similarly, if we are dividing the octave into so many parts, no two adjacent parts will span the same number of frequencies.

Let's now look at a musical keyboard. Take an octave, from the notes C to C is 8, as shown. We've found that it sounds right to divide the octave into seven, the notes being identified by the letters of the alphabet. If we work to our reference A = 440 cycles per second, we find that for the notes to sound 'exactly right' they have to have the frequencies indicated. This is known as the "Just Intonated Scale". The problem with having a justly intonated seven note scale is that it is impossible to transpose a piece of music. Say the piece was pitched a little too low to match a particular singer's range, then by shifting up a tone (C to D, B to C, etc,) would lead to totally incorrect intervals between notes. Consequently it was necessary to re-split the scale, and it was found that a certain 12-tone scale fitted the bill exactly. The extra notes are:

Set between C and D (C sharp or D flat)
Set between D and E (D sharp or E flat)
Set between F and G (F sharp or G flat)
Set between G and A (G sharp or A flat)
Set between A and B (A sharp or B flat)

Unfortunately it is the way of the justly intonated scale that the C sharp of a piece played in one key doesn't exactly correspond in frequency to D flat when played in another. The problem isn't insurmountable for an instrument such as a violin, where the musician "makes" the notes as he plays the instrument; but for a keyboard player who actually has to rely on preset pitches it is impossible to switch from one key to another when playing an instrument tuned with just intonation. So a new concept evolved, that of the equally tempered scale, which saved the day, especially when electronic musical instruments came on the scene.

Why? Because when dealing with electronic systems it makes real sense to divide the octave into twelve equal steps, with the semi-tone – the gap between each note – remaining a constant factor.

Let's put this theory into a graphical format.

EQUAL TEMPERED SCALE	261.62Hz	293.66Hz	329.62Hz	349.22Hz	392.00Hz	440.00Hz	493.88Hz	523.25Hz
JUST INTONATION	264.00Hz	297.00Hz	330.00Hz	352.00Hz	396.00Hz	440.00Hz	495.00Hz	528.00Hz
DIFFERENCE	2.38Hz	3.34Hz	0.38Hz	2.78Hz	4.00Hz		1.12Hz	4.75Hz

9

Figure 9 shows the two scale systems, 'just intonation' and 'equal temperament', and you can compare the relative frequency values between the two conventions.

Timbre:

Timbre is the quality of a sound that enables the listener to distinguish it from another of the same pitch. The timbre or tone colour of a note depends on the actual shape of the waveform produced. If we return to our example of the sine wave produced by the vibrating tuning fork, we see how the compressions and rarefactions of the air determine the shape of the waveform produced. Look now at the way in which the air particles have lined up in figure 10 below.

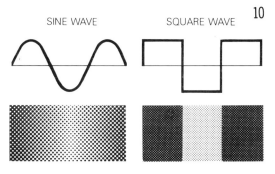

SINE WAVE   SQUARE WAVE   10

PARTICLE DENSITY

The source of the sound is such that the particles are compressed to a certain density for a set period of time before being rarefied for an equal period.

This waveform is known as a square wave. The wave still travels at the same speed (the speed of sound), so if it is of the same wavelength, the ear will interpret its pitch as being the same. But because the air particles are vibrating in a different manner, the ear will perceive its sound to have a totally different tonal colour.

Unlike pitch, there is no simple quantitive measurement of timbre. The only way to express this parameter is to describe the waveform produced. This is all very well for simple shapes, such as the two we've already mentioned, but since just a small variation can make a considerable difference to the timbre the ear perceives, then a more satisfactory method of describing this parameter is necessary.

A waveshape can be defined by means of a mathematical equation, but to most of us, this is more an academic exercise than of any practical use.

Loudness

The concept of loudness is, on the surface, a relatively simple one to grasp. Two sounds may have the same pitch and timbre, but it is possible still to distinguish between them if one sounds very loud, and the other very soft.

How does this relate to our compression and rarefaction of air particles concept?

Consider the square wave example illustrated in figure 10. Here we have two states of existence:

1 Compression – whereby the density of the air particles abruptly becomes much greater than the average air density, and it stays at this constant value for half the cycle.

2 Rarefaction – when the density becomes less than the average, and there are fewer particles present per given area.

Now the loudness of the sound is governed by the relative amounts by which these densities vary. In figure 11 we see three examples of this:

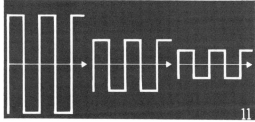

11

The wavelength and waveshapes remain the same, only the variations in air densities are different, and the greater the difference the louder we perceive the sound. The greater the peaks and troughs, the greater the amplitude, or loudness.

When listening to music, loudness isn't as simple as loud and soft. There's much more to it. When considering a sound the dynamics (or changes in loudness) are a vital aspect of the way in which we interpret the sound.

Listen to the sound produced by playing a single note on a piano. Depress a key. As the hammer strikes the string, the output of the piano rises from zero, to a maximum level almost instantaneously (figure 12).

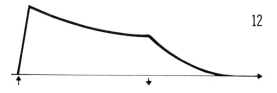

12

The sound then starts to die away gradually as the vibration of the strings is damped by the friction of the air. The key is then released, causing the piano's dampers to deaden the strings, and the note starts to die away fairly rapidly until all is quiet again. So during this whole procedure the amplitude has been continually changing. The shape which is traced out by the amplitude is known as the envelope and were this envelope to be different from that described, the sound wouldn't be like that of a piano.

Periodic and Aperiodic Waveshapes

Don't be put off by this heading, because this is a very straightforward idea. We mentioned above how the shape of the amplitude of a note played on the piano is known as the envelope. Now this is a waveform. It has a particular shape traced out by the way in which the output volume changes over a period of time. This is known as an aperiodic waveform. Why? Because it doesn't constantly repeat itself – some event has to happen before it can re-occur; in this case the event is the playing of the note again.

Periodic waveforms are constantly repeating themselves, i.e. cycling round. As a result, if they were occurring within the audio spectrum (the range of human hearing) and you were listening to them, they would have a definite discernible pitch. And of course the rate at which they repeat themselves is their frequency.

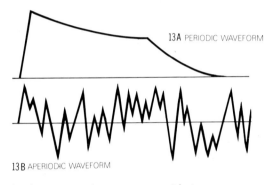

13A PERIODIC WAVEFORM

13B APERIODIC WAVEFORM

In these examples we are considering a very slow waveform – the aperiodic envelope, and a much faster one, that of an audible tone. But there are other types of such aperiodic waveforms.

Look at figure 13. Here we see a single extremely complex looking waveform. It is shooting all over the place, but as you can see it doesn't repeat itself. Therefore it cannot be considered as a periodic waveform. This waveform is made up of a random combination of hundreds of pitches, and if we listened to it we would perceive a hissing sound with virtually no vestige of recognisable pitch.

Natural examples of such aperiodic waveforms are made by wind, or waves crashing on a beach.

The Human Ear and Sound

The three elements of sound described above are nice tidy concepts, all of which can be neatly evaluated mathematically. But then along we come with our ears, the receivers of the sound, and unfortunately (due to the limitations of the

response of our ears) we have to make certain allowances when dealing with raw sound.

Our ears function rather like the speakers of a hi-fi system in reverse. The compressions and rarefactions of any sound that reaches our ears cause a small membrane to vibrate back and forth.

This vibration is detected by a series of small hairs contained within our inner ear. These generate a minute signal which is transmitted *via* our nervous system to the brain, and, hey-presto, we hear noises. In essence it's very simple but, like a hi-fi system, our ears have limitations as to the "quality" and range of sounds to which they can respond.

Pitch and the Human Ear

Our ears will respond only to frequencies within a certain range, known as the Audible Frequency Spectrum. Why? Because the actual mechanism of the ear can operate only within a certain range. But even the best microphones cannot detect sounds as efficiently as the human ear.

Generally speaking the frequencies in a healthy young adult can detect ranges from between 18-25 Hz up to around 20,000 Hz, which in musical terms is around a ten octave span – wider than virtually all acoustic musical instruments, with the possible exception of the pipe organ. As with all parts of the body, age takes its toll, and the audible span of frequencies decreases, most notably towards the top end of the spectrum.

When considering the audible frequency spectrum, it should be remembered that we are dealing with pure tones (sine waves). We could obviously detect a square wave of 10 Hz, because it incorporates tones of 30, 50, 70 Hz etc. (the harmonics).

It is also important to note that the ear doesn't respond linearly to all frequencies across the audio spectrum. Figure 14 shows a typical frequency response plot for the ear.

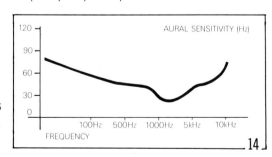

AURAL SENSITIVITY (Hz)

FREQUENCY

14

You can see that it isn't simply a case of being able to hear frequencies of 21 Hz, but not those of 19 Hz. The amplitude that we perceive the sound to be decreases as we approach the boundary of the audio spectrum, just like the response characteristic of a hi-fi speaker or microphone.

Timbre, Loudness and the Human Ear

As a corollary we find that the ear is more sensitive to some frequencies than to others, and this also depends on the strength of the sound falling on the ear drum.

This makes things yet more complicated, because as the ear doesn't respond in a constant manner to different frequencies, then it follows that we will perceive sounds with different timbres but of identical pitch and amplitude, as being of different loudness. This is a quirk of the human ear, but one we don't have to worry about too much at this stage.

Resonance

In nature, we find that a lot of things have their own rhythm. A child on a swing rocks back and forth at a fixed rate. He might be able to swing higher or lower, but not at a faster or slower rate (try it next time you're in a park and there's no-one about). Similarly, a clock's pendulum traces out a path in an exact period of time – the only way to change this is to alter the length of the chain supporting the weight. This natural frequency of oscillation occurs everywhere. Consider ringing a church bell – this time we're concerned with the way in which the bell rings, not the actual sound it makes.

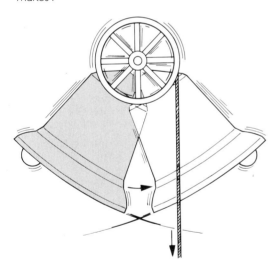

Church bells are heavy pieces of metal, and there's no way you can instantly move an object weighing maybe several tons. The bell on its mechanism has what is known as an inertia, and you have to build up a supply of energy to get it moving before it will sound. We get the bell moving initially by tugging on a rope. The bell moves a little from its resting place but the more it moves the more it is trying to 'centre' itself, i.e. return to its position of rest. So we have to release the rope, and it swings back to its original position; but because it is such a massive object it overshoots the resting point, at which time we give the rope another pull injecting another package of energy to move

the bell just a little further from rest. The process then repeats itself and we find that we eventually get the bell moving enough for the clapper to strike the bell.

Now it is essential that we inject the packages of energy, i.e. pull on the rope, at exactly the right instant otherwise we will be helping to retard the bell's movement rather than increase it.

But we don't have to pull on every swing. We could pull every second swing, or every third swing, and although our efforts would not be quite so effective, we would still be contributing positively to the bell's motion.

So the rocking bell has its own natural frequency of oscillation, or resonant frequency.

The resonant frequency is defined as being that frequency at which a certain body wants to oscillate.

Loudspeaker cabinets tend to have resonant frequencies. When you feed in a signal to be amplified at that frequency, the cabinet finds it much easier to move the air particles and you find that the speaker boosts the levels of sounds at this frequency much more. Speaker cabinets usually have a resonant frequency around 50- 60 Hz, but, naturally, manufacturers try to prevent this phenomenon occurring as it corrupts the performance of the unit.

Natural Harmonic Series

Closely allied to the subject of Resonance is that of the natural harmonic series.

The sine wave that we encountered when using the tuning fork is considered to be the most basic waveshape. It cannot be broken down into a simpler form, i.e. no two other more basic shapes can be summed to produce a sine wave. However, we can produce other waveforms by adding together sine waves of different frequencies and amplitudes.

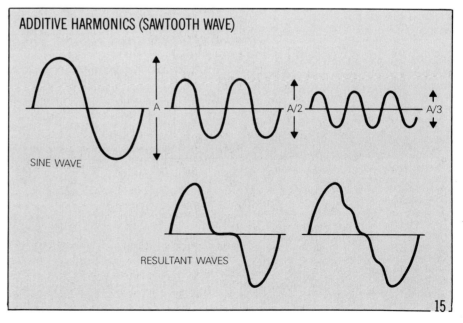

ADDITIVE HARMONICS (SAWTOOTH WAVE)

SINE WAVE

RESULTANT WAVES

15

Generally speaking the sine wave with the lowest frequency is known as the root or fundamental, and it is this that gives the sound its basic pitch. The other sine waves used to construct the sound are known as overtones. Most acoustic sounds tend to have overtones that bear a direct mathematical relationship to the fundamental and hence to one another. These are known as harmonics.

The harmonic series consists of pure tones that are simple multiples of the fundamental. So, say we have an oscillation of frequency F, this is the fundamental or first harmonic. The second harmonic has a frequency of 2 x F, the third 3 x F, and so on. Say the fundamental frequency (F) was 100 Hz, then the second harmonic would be 200 Hz, the seventh Harmonic 700 Hz, the twenty-fifth Harmonic 2500 Hz and so on. So you can see that the harmonic spectrum can incorporate many different frequencies and still be within the audio spectrum.

If we were listening to the sound of a 'cello string which is pitched at C (roughly 132 cycles per second), and we were to closely examine the composition of that sound we would find that the strongest element would be a sine wave of 132 Hz, and that there were also frequencies of 264, 396, 528 Hz etc. That is to say that if 132 Hz were the root frequency, f, then in addition we would find sine waves of varying amplitudes at frequencies of 2xf, 3xf, 4xf, etc. We could represent the relative amplitudes of the harmonics as shown.

Now look at figure 16. What we've got here is a pure sine wave. Its actual frequency doesn't matter, but let's call it 100 Hz (say), and of amplitude 'I'. Now if we add to it another sine wave oscillating at three times its frequency (i.e. 300 Hz) but only a third of its size then we get a resultant 2. Add another sine wave five times the frequency (500 Hz) but of magnitude a fifth, and we get 3. Can you see that this is starting to look like a square wave? And if we were to add more and more sine waves of multiple frequencies and divisive amplitudes, we would eventually get a perfect square wave.

The multiples are the harmonic – the 1st –100 Hz, the third – 300 Hz, the fifth – 500 Hz etc. This can be depicted graphically.

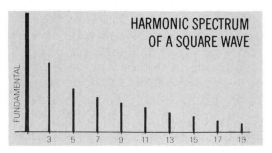

HARMONIC SPECTRUM OF A SQUARE WAVE

One of the first instruments to utilise this "addition of sine waves" concept to generate different sounds was the Hammond tone-wheel organ. Here a myriad of waveforms was produced by combining harmonics in differing proportion. Eight harmonically related volume controls (drawbars) were used to introduce the sine wave tones. The top Hammonds boasted nine different harmonics per note, and they calculated that over 100 million possible timbral permutations were possible using this system. Figure 17 .

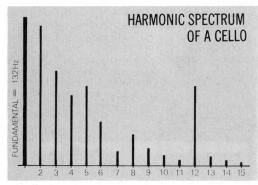

HARMONIC SPECTRUM OF A CELLO

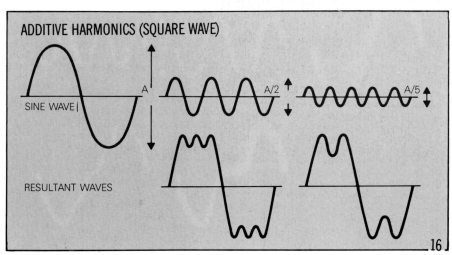

ADDITIVE HARMONICS (SQUARE WAVE)

SINE WAVE

RESULTANT WAVES

16

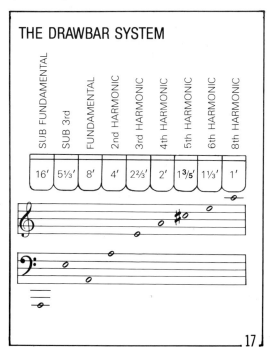

THE DRAWBAR SYSTEM

17

Waveforms

We have already introduced the concept of
waveforms when discussing periodic/aperiodic
waveshapes (p.12). A waveform is a convenient
method of describing a basic tone. And of course
it can be constructed by adding together sine
waves of different frequencies and amplitudes.

There are five main waveforms that you will
regularly encounter: Sine, Square, Pulse,
Triangle, and Sawtooth. When describing a
waveform, we aren't particularly concerned
with its frequency. A sine wave may oscillate at
5 Hz or 5000 Hz – it's still a sine wave. Within
the confines of this book we will be dealing with
waveshapes lying not only within the audible
frequency spectrum, but also at sub-audio
frequencies (oscillations below the lower
threshold of human hearing). This is because
these waveforms are also used as control signals
for 'modulating' sounds. More of this later.

The Sine Wave

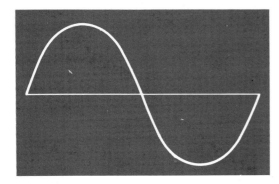

Sine waves are the fundamental sound element,
but up until recently they have been expensive
and awkward to generate electronically. Today's
technology has solved many of these problems
and the sine wave has become the workhorse
in many contemporary synthesizers and
computer music facilities.

SHAPE: You can see by looking at the sine
wave's shape that it has a smooth contour
which gives rise to its pure clean tone.

SPECTRUM: The harmonic spectrum of a sine
wave is simply the fundamental.

SOUND: The sine wave has a flute-like
character. Very clear, and clean.

The Square Wave

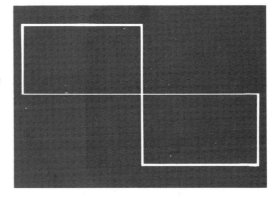

The square wave is quite the simplest of
waveforms to generate. The figure above shows
the waveform really exists only in two states –
high and low (on or off). In fact, simply by
flicking a light switch on and off we are
effectively making a square wave.

SHAPE: A simple hi-low transition, but often
one will encounter a "square" wave with
rounded corners, which means that some of
the higher frequency harmonics are missing.

SPECTRUM: The formula for a square wave is
$F + 3F/3 + 5F/5 + 7F/7$ . . . etc. and this
translates to the graphical representation
shown. Obviously it is the lower numbered
harmonics that play the major part in
determining the shape, and hence timbral
quality of the waveform, but as stated the
presence of the higher harmonics gives rise to
the sharpened corners.

SOUND: A square wave has a mellow hollow
sounding quality to it, very much like that of
the clarinet, the similarities being particularly
those of the dominant odd harmonics, which
give the square wave its characteristic nasal
timbre.

The Pulse Wave

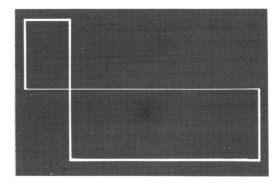

Often known as the rectangular wave, this is a
variation of the square wave.

SHAPE: Again the waveform exists in just two
states, high or low; but this time the relative

proportions of the two states are not the same. To express the exact shape of the pulse wave we generally give it a percentage value to express the relative amounts of the two phases, or duty cycle as it is known. The figure on p. 15 illustrates this.

As you can see, a square wave has a 50% duty cycle, and a 20% pulse wave spends 2/10ths of its time in a high state, and 8/10ths in a low one.

SPECTRUM: A typical harmonic spectrum plot of a pulse wave is shown in the figure below. The exact amplitudes of the harmonics depend on the specific shape of the waveform, but in comparison to the square wave, you can see that the even harmonics have been strengthened.

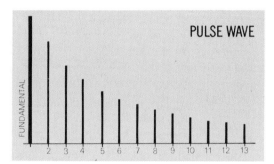

SOUND: The pulse wave has a characteristic reedy, nasal quality to it, and becomes increasingly thin the further the duty cycle deviates from the central 50% value. To the listener, a 5% pulse wave sounds exactly the same as a 95% one.

The pulse waveform has become an increasingly important device with the revolution in digital technology. You can specify a number using the duty cycle of a pulse wave. So by constantly varying the duty cycle we can transmit information very efficiently.

The Triangle Wave

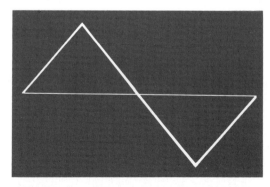

SHAPE: A triangle wave has a somewhat similar shape to a sine wave, but instead of a continually changing curve, it utilises straight lines.

SPECTRUM: These discrepancies are accounted for by the presence of odd harmonics in small amounts.

The magnitude of these harmonics decreases exponentially so that the 9th harmonic (say) is present in a ratio of 1:81 with the fundamental.

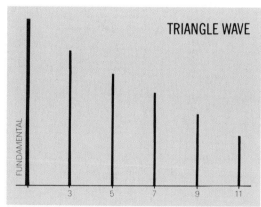

SOUND: The triangle wave, like the sine wave, has a similar pure clarity to it. But the presence of those extra odd harmonics does make it sound brighter than its 'smooth' benefactor, and to many ears the sound is more pleasing.

The Sawtooth Wave

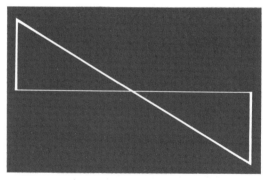

There are two kinds of sawtooth wave – ramp up, and ramp down, but in the audio spectrum both sound exactly the same as they have the same harmonic content and are mirror images of one another.

SHAPE: On first appearance, the sawtooth wave looks very similar to the triangle wave, but you will notice that upon reaching a maximum, or minimum, level the waveform 'resets', and returns instantly to its initial position.

SPECTRUM: The sawtooth wave is predominant in neither odd nor even harmonics, the harmonics die away at a steady rate.

SOUND: The sawtooth waveform, being rich in harmonics, is a very bright full sounding waveform. It has a particular brassy quality to it.

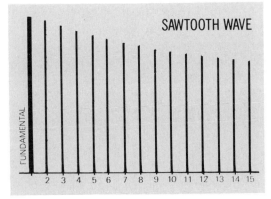

SAWTOOTH WAVE

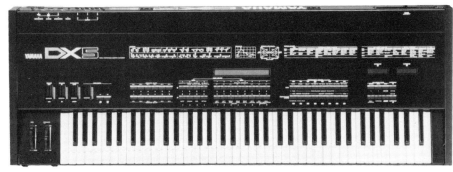

ONE OF THE NEW BREED OF FM SYNTHESIZERS

Harmonics and the Musical Stave

We've seen that the natural harmonic series utilises multiples of the fundamental frequency, but this can be illustrated with respect to musical nomenclature.

Figure 18 shows a musical stave. If we take as our fundamental frequency a note pitched two octaves below middle C (65.4 Hz to be exact), then the harmonics of the natural series fall on the notes as shown.

Understanding the workings of the natural harmonic progression is valuable in all forms of electronic music synthesis, but especially so in understanding the more recent advances in FM digital synthesis which utilises the summation and modulation of sine waves.

Overtones

So far we have discussed only tones that are produced by adding together multiples of the fundamental frequency. These are commonplace when considering musical instruments, but many naturally occurring sounds incorporate pitches of frequencies that do not form part of the natural harmonic series.

In a musical context the most obvious examples of this category are clangorous sounds such as bells, glockenspiels, cowbells, gongs etc. Generally speaking there is still a relationship between the tones used to construct these sounds, but they don't fall neatly into the simple multiple variety. You may find that the waveform produced by a ringing bell utilises tones that have frequencies 7/3, or 13/2 (say) that of the fundamental. So if the fundamental were 100 Hz, these examples would represent frequencies of 233.3 Hz and 650 Hz. A tone that isn't a whole-number-multiple of the fundamental frequency is known as an overtone.

Figure (right) shows the make-up of the spectrum of such an enharmonic sound.

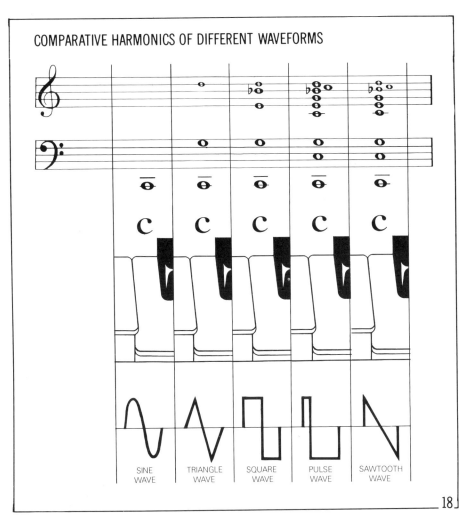

COMPARATIVE HARMONICS OF DIFFERENT WAVEFORMS

SINE WAVE   TRIANGLE WAVE   SQUARE WAVE   PULSE WAVE   SAWTOOTH WAVE

18

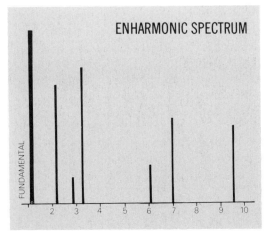

ENHARMONIC SPECTRUM

Noise

In some instances, especially when considering certain percussive instruments, it is impossible to ascertain exactly the pitch of the fundamental frequency, and consequently the sound appears to have no definite pitch.

This can be taken a stage further. Imagine the case of a sound made up of all possible frequencies within the audio spectrum, and the amplitudes of each frequency randomly changing from zero to a relative maximum value. What would you hear? The answer is a totally unpitched hissing sound, much like the sound you hear when you tune between FM stations on your radio. This sound is known as noise, and it is a very useful tool in electronic music synthesis – especially subtractive synthesis.

Noise can be used as an audio mask. If in a certain environment you produce a continuous level of noise, it will tend to obliterate all other sounds. The noise signal, as it incorporates all frequencies, will tend to obliterate any other more simple harmonic structures.

There are various categories of noise, generally designated in terms of their colour – white, pink, azure, etc. These arise from the amount of "randomness" in the amplitude of the frequencies. This aspect of noise is dealt with in a later chapter.

What is Electricity?

The actual "mechanics" of electricity bear, for many of our intents and purposes, a strong allegiance to those of sound. And as with the theory of sound, we do need to know a little about electricity and electronics to get the most from electronic music synthesis.

There is a difference between electrics and electronics. Electrical engineering is generally the study of electricity in relation to power. We use electricity for heat, light, locomotion, and more; and in these fields large amounts of electricity are used.

Electronics, on the other hand, is the use of electricity as a means of controlling things. We could use the analogy of the human body. Our brain sends and receives nervous pulses from all over our body telling us to move our arm, or that the eye can see a brick wall coming towards us at great speed, etc. The nervous signals correspond to an electronic system. When we have to actually move our arm we need to call upon some form of energy to cause our muscles to operate. The work energy, in our analogy, can be considered the 'electrics'.

Another way of looking at it is to consider a hi-fi system. Take for example the tuner and the amplifier. The tuner translates radio waves into a very low power signal which is of little use

to us as it is. The tuner is an electronic device. When this signal is fed to a power amplifier, the signal's strength is multiplied many times, to such a degree that there is sufficient power to move the cones of the speakers, and we hear the programme. The amplifier is the electrical component.

In an electronic musical instrument we are simply processing small control signals to provide a final signal which, when fed through amplifier and speakers, produces (hopefully) the desired sound.

But there have been electric and electronic musical instruments over the years – what's the difference?

The easiest way to answer this is by considering the electric and electronic pianos. In the early part of this century, designers had perfected the audio amplifier, and wanted to apply it to musical instruments. The obvious way to make a piano louder was to put a microphone or some kind of pick-up near the strings, and simply amplify the sound produced. This in essence is an electric piano. Variations on the structure of the piano were made, so that the instrument bore little resemblance to the original article. But an electric piano always took a mechanically vibrating medium (be it string, rod, or metal reed), and turned it into an electrical signal by means of a transducer (microphone or pick-up). An electronic piano, on the other hand, utilises no mechanical devices to generate the pitches of the notes. Instead, all the tones are generated by means of electronic devices (solid state circuitry as it used to be known), and the final output signal is fed to an amplifier and speaker accordingly.

Electricity is a type of energy that is transmitted by the movement of electrons down a conductor – a piece of wire for example.

One of the best ways to understand the concept of electricity is to use an analogy with a hydro-electric dam.

Here water is stored in a reservoir. To supply power, it is released from a higher level and allowed to flow to a lower one *via* a turbine, and as it flows through the turbine it rotates the mechanism and power is eventually created. So, the water in the reservoir has a potential to do work by virtue of its height above the turbine. This is known as its potential energy.

Now electricity flows in a similar fashion, but instead of flowing from a higher to a lower level, it moves from higher to lower electrical potential. Consider a simple circuit of a battery driving a small bulb.

The two terminals of the battery are analogous to the two levels of the reservoir, and the bulb equates to the turbine in between.

When the circuit is complete then the

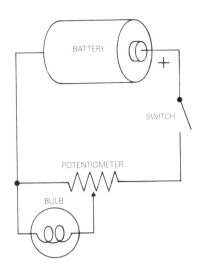

電électrons in the circuit can flow from the battery terminal of higher potential to the lower.

As the electrons move around the circuit they are channelled through the bulb which draws energy from the flow of electrons. This energy manifests itself as heat and light.

Eventually the potential between the two terminals of the battery will become less and less until there is not enough potential to cause the electrons to flow around the circuit, and consequently the bulb fails to light. This is similar to the situation when all the water has been drained from the top reservoir, and there is no potential height difference left.

So the concept of electricity relates to the flow of electrons in metals that are conductive or semi-conductive.

Say we were listening to pure sine wave tone emanating from a loudspeaker. The

vibration of the loudspeaker's cone is setting up compressions and rarefactions in the air particles, and the signal wave is thus transmitted through the air to the listener at the speed of sound. But what is it that is causing the loudspeaker to move back and forth?

In the simplest terms it is the electrical signal that is being applied to the two terminals of the loudspeaker. And the actual movement of the electric signal applied to the speaker corresponds directly to the waveforms set up in the air particles. So to originate a sine wave from the loudspeaker it is necessary to apply an electrical sine wave signal to the terminals of the speaker.

Electrical Measurements

There are three main units of electrical and electronic measurement – voltage, current and resistance.

VOLTAGE: The voltage is the electrical potential between two points, it equates to the height of the head of water in our hydro-electric example. Voltage is measured in volts.

RESISTANCE: This measurement specifies the way in which the conductor down which the electrons are travelling restricts their flow. In the hydro-scheme example, the rate of flow of water down through the pipe to the turbine is dependent on the thickness of the pipe, the thinner the pipe the greater the resistance, and the less current of water that can be used.

When dealing with an electrical circuit, the various components in the circuit tend to prevent the easy flow of electrons.

CURRENT: Current is the amount of electricity flowing in a conductor. So if we have a fixed head of water (voltage) the amount of water flowing (current) depends on the thickness of the pipes (the resistance). Current is measured in amperes (amps).

A fourth unit is the watt. This is a unit of power, and can be obtained from the value of the current and voltage: wattage = current x voltage.

Probably the most useful unit to consider throughout this book is that of voltage – the potential electrical difference between two points.

Remember, like sound, the electrons flowing down a conductor all travel at exactly the same velocity, in this case the speed of light – around 186,000 miles per second.

Electrical Oscillators
An electrical oscillator is one in which the electrons flow first in one direction and then another. So an electrical square wave generator would equate to a battery where the terminals were continually being reversed at a fixed rate. The electrons would thus instantaneously move in one direction and then the other.

Reversing terminals is not a satisfactory method of creating an alternating voltage, and consequently electrical components are used to form oscillating circuits which fulfil such specific tasks.

AC/DC
We now need to introduce the concept of direct and alternating currents. The example of our battery illustrates a direct current situation. The potential between the two points remains a constant, a steady constant – 9 volts (say). This is known as a direct current (dc).

The situation whereby the terminals were effectively reversing is known as an alternating current, although usually such a signal alternates smoothly as a sine wave, not a square wave. The most apparent example of an AC source is the domestic electricity supply – the mains. Here the output from a wall outlet is varying 50 or 60 times a second, and the variation is defined by a sine wave.

AC signals do not have to be at mains voltage, nor does a DC signal have to be a mere handful of volts potential – these are just examples.

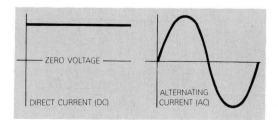

Analogue and Digital
There are two main types of signal that have to be considered: analogue and digital. You've probably heard both these terms before, the difference between them is a very simple one. The figure below shows a bulb and a battery connected in a circuit. Also as part of the circuit are a switch and a potentiometer – a device that can be used to vary the voltage. The whole circuit operates rather like a domestic light dimmer.

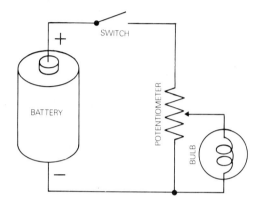

The battery dictates the maximum voltage we deal with, so we can draw in the power rails at 0 and 9 volts (shown below). The potentiometer varies the voltage across the light bulb, hence its brightness will vary.

This type of circuit is known as an analogue one in which you can use the rheostat to change the voltage applied to the bulb to any value between zero and nine volts (the power rails).

If we remove the potentiometer and use the switch, we can only have the bulb full on or full off. This is the simplest kind of digital circuit, where everything can exist in only one of two states 'on' or 'off' (or 'high' and 'low'). In this situation the analogue system has the advantage of being more useful as the bulb brightness can be continually varied.

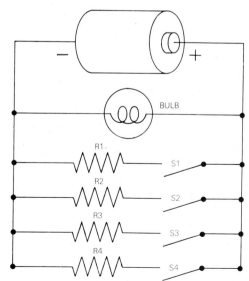

Now we have four switches which are connected up in conjunction with four resistors. A resistor is a device that restricts the flow of current (the amount of electricity), so as switch one (SI) is closed some of the current is diverted away from the bulb, consequently it dims a bit; if S2 is then closed, the bulb dims a bit more and so on. So we have a degree of control over the brightness of the bulb by means of specifying 'Ons' and 'Offs'.

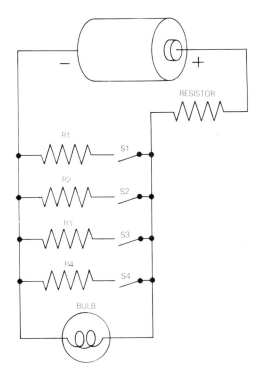

This circuit above is a good deal more complicated because we've introduced different values of resistors. So as switch 1 (SI) is closed half the current flows through the bulb, half through resistor RI. If S2 only is closed a quarter of the current flows through R2, and three quarters through the bulb. S3 and R3 drain off one-eighth, and S4 and R4 one-sixteenth. So by using various combinations of these switches, we can vary the brightness of the bulb from 1/16 to full power in one-sixteenth steps as per the following table:

Switch	1	2	3	4	Brightness
	*OFF	OFF	OFF	OFF	1
	OFF	OFF	OFF	ON	15/16
	OFF	OFF	ON	OFF	7/8
	OFF	OFF	ON	ON	13/16
	*OFF	ON	OFF	OFF	3/4
	OFF	ON	OFF	ON	11/16
	OFF	ON	ON	OFF	5/8
	OFF	ON	ON	ON	9/16
	*ON	OFF	OFF	OFF	1/2
	ON	OFF	OFF	ON	7/16
	ON	OFF	ON	OFF	3/8
	ON	OFF	ON	ON	5/16
	*ON	ON	OFF	OFF	1/4
	ON	ON	OFF	ON	3/16
	ON	ON	ON	OFF	1/8
	ON	ON	ON	ON	1/16

So, from expressing the settings of four digital devices (S1-4) we can specify a parameter (the bulb's brightness in this case) to an accuracy of 1/16 (6.25%). If you look closely you can see that by switching on just SI you are switching from full brightness to half power, whereas S4 makes a difference to the brightness of just 1/16. In this example we call SI the most significant element, and S4 the least significant.

You can see that if we had only two switches, we would be able to vary the bulb's brilliance in steps of one quarter (indicated by the starred entries in the above table). It follows therefore that we can say that the definition we can achieve increases drastically with the number of 'switches' we employ. Mathematically this corresponds to "two to the power of the number of 'switches' involved". In the above example we have four switches so we could expect '2 to the power of 4', i.e. $2 \times 2 \times 2 \times 2 = 16$ possible settings. If we'd used eight switches we could have defined the brightness to an accuracy of '2 to the power 8', which is 256 or 0.39%.

Digital circuitry is all about numbers. And the number system is different from the one we normally use. It is called binary, and naturally uses only two basic digits 0 and 1 (representing on and off or high and low). So in binary the numbers 0 to 7 would be: 0,1,10,11,100,101,110,111. If you take 0 to be OFF and 1 to be ON then this follows the patterns of the above table.

Signal and Noise

You might think that it is much better to be able to fully vary a parameter as you could with an analogue circuit, not having to rely just on stepped values. And in many circumstances this would be so, but in audio circuits several facets make digital circuitry extremely attractive. For example, we generally have a continual problem – that of background noise. Every element in an electronic circuit causes a small amount of noise.

Think about recording using a cassette tape recorder; this is an analogue device. During quiet passages you are aware of a degree of tape hiss in the background. There are ways to reduce this noise, but you will never totally eliminate it. But if you were just recording numbers that represented the music, the noise wouldn't matter, because it wouldn't affect the value of the numbers, and when translated back into an audio signal there would be virtually no noise present in the signal.

Similarly, when creating sounds as in synthesis, you may find that a digital system can give you a cleaner, purer sound – but we shall be considering this more fully later.

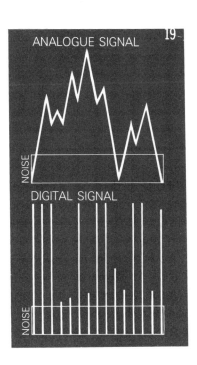

Digital: Bits and Bandwidths

As shown, digital systems enable sound to be expressed as a series of numbers. The fidelity of the sound depends on two factors – the length of the word and the number of words per given space of time, for example, a sampling device generally utilises at least 12 bit words, i.e. binary numbers consisting of 12 digits. The frequency of words relates directly to the bandwidth or frequency span of the sound. In simpler terms, the more information used to specify the sound the better its quality.

This becomes particularly important when using "Sampling" machines which take digital recordings of actual sounds and, by a system of digital number manipulation, use them as a sound source which can be transposed into any key. Thus the sound can be played at any pitch when using some form of controller such as a keyboard.

COMPACT DISC PLAYER

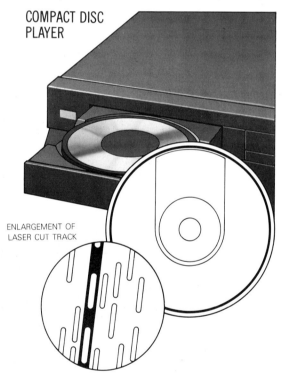

ENLARGEMENT OF LASER CUT TRACK

A compact disc also stores sound in the form of digital numbers, and here the fidelity required is much greater, and CD players have specifications that boast 16 bit words and 20kHz bandwidth.

Digital Memories

In a digital system information has to be stored and the devices used for this purpose are known as memories. The amount of memory to store a one second sound is considerable – if the bandwidth of the sound is, say, 10kHz (10,000 cycles per second) then 20,000 bytes (digital words), are required for every second

DX7 CARTRIDGE PORT

of that sound. So, every second of a compact disc requires 40k bytes of memory – thus a 40 minute recording needs 96 million bytes of information (96,000k bytes). A compact disc is known as a ROM – read only memory, and as such is a relatively cheap memory storage medium. If silicon chips were used the price would be astronomic.

Synthesizers don't store the actual digital translation of a sound, but use the digital memory to store the data required to produce that sound. This is similar in a way to representing a house by means of a set of plans – give a person a set of plans and materials and he can build a house; if you store the various settings of all the parameters required to make up a sound then you can produce the specific desired effect with the instrument for which the data was intended.

VOICES

The first thing we should establish is that when we are considering 'voices' generally we aren't referring to the human voice.

A voice can be described as a single sound source. For example, a clarinet is just one voice in an orchestra. It is capable of producing just one sound at any instant in time. The human voice can also, of course, be considered as a 'voice', but for our purposes it doesn't hold a monopoly on the term.

So a voice is a single sound source. To what then does the term 'voicing' refer? The voicing is the actual quality of the sound – its tone colour, shape etc. A clarinet has a different voicing from that of an oboe, etc. So when we are discussing the voicing of a sound we are referring to its tonal make-up.

Confusion often occurs between these two terms, but these definitions should establish the differences between them.

Monophonic and Polyphonic

The clarinet as mentioned above can produce only one sound at any instant in time. By its very design, you can specify only one pitch (by covering the specific holes in the body of the instrument), thus you can play only single notes. All woodwind and brass instruments can play only single notes, and our human voices are capable of producing only single notes. All these single voice instruments are known as monophonic sources.

A piano, on the other hand, is capable of producing many notes at a single time. If you put the sustain pedal on and quickly run a finger up the keyboard you can get pretty well every set of strings (every voice) producing a sound – though it will sound awful! An instrument such as a piano, a pipe organ, a vibraphone etc. that has a separate tone producing element (in the case of the piano – the strings), and trigger mechanism (separate keys) for each note within its range is known as a fully polyphonic instrument.

There are certain anomalies in the world of the acoustic instrument that fall outside this neat categorization. For example, you can bow two strings of the violin simultaneously and you can strum all six strings of the guitar virtually at once.

In the world of electronic music there are two distinct varieties of synthesizer –

monophonic and polyphonic, but the latter section is somewhat more involved.

Monophonic Synthesizers

The monophonic synthesizer was, essentially, the first on the scene. Why? Because it is the simplest to design and build. All that is necessary is to have an electronic circuit capable of producing the desired sound, and by means of a simple keyboard controller you can give that single sound the desired pitch.

The first commercial synthesizers of the late 1960s utilised voltage control for setting up all

1 a single voice monophonic synthesizer can only produce a single note at any instant in time.
2 With separate voice modules for each key the fully polyphonic synthesizer can produce as many notes at a given instant as desired.
3 To cut the cost of having a voice module for each key, a system of voice sharing has evolved. In this way a certain number of voices (usually between 4-16) are assigned to whatever notes are being played on the keyboard.

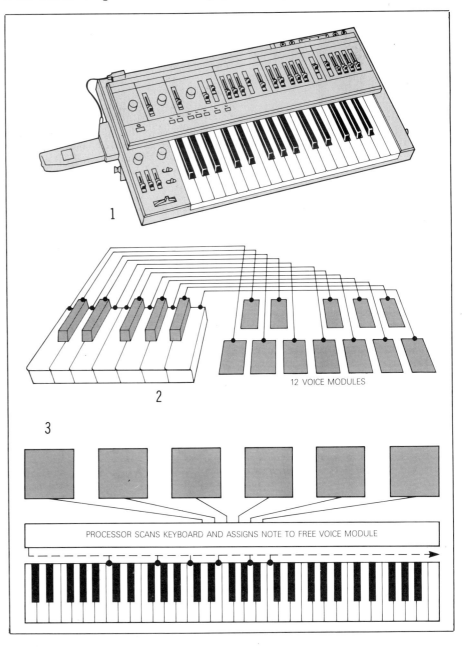

1

2

12 VOICE MODULES

3

PROCESSOR SCANS KEYBOARD AND ASSIGNS NOTE TO FREE VOICE MODULE

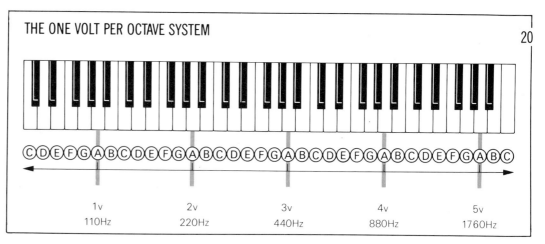

THE ONE VOLT PER OCTAVE SYSTEM

20

| 1v | 2v | 3v | 4v | 5v |
| 110Hz | 220Hz | 440Hz | 880Hz | 1760Hz |

the parameters. So if the bottom note of the keyboard produced zero volts, a note one octave up produced a I volt signal, 2 octaves up produced 2 volts and so on, then the voltage derived from the keyboard could be correlated to the pitch of the note to be produced. This is a simple, neat system, but of course you can specify only a single note at a time.

The monophonic synthesizer's prime role is, naturally enough, as a soloing instrument, or for bass lines, where the restriction of single notes is not a handicap. And of course the monophonic synthesizer could be multi-tracked

in the studio (i.e. a full score could be recorded one part at a time), this technique being the domain of such great synthesists as Walter Carlos and Isao Tomita.

This type of synthesizer will always have a role to play, because, although it may seem of limited use, in terms of cost it offers far more sound shaping circuitry. Originally the polyphonic synthesizer was around three to five times the price of its monophonic counterpart. Today a comparable 'poly' costs virtually twice the price of its monophonic compatriate but such a comparison isn't always possible.

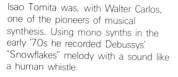
Isao Tomita was, with Walter Carlos, one of the pioneers of musical synthesis. Using mono synths in the early '70s he recorded Debussys' "Snowflakes" melody with a sound like a human whistle.

The monophonic synthesizer also has an expressive quality that cannot truly be matched by its polyphonic counterpart.

A synthesizer is by definition an instrument that can create sound/sounds by specifying the basic elements of pitch, timbre, and amplitude – all three of which can vary over the period the note (or sound) exists. As we shall find when discussing performance controls, these three elements can be varied by the player while the notes are actually sounding – so we can introduce vibrato as would a violinist, we can bend the pitch of a note as would a guitarist, we can create overblow effects as would a flautist. But this can only effectively be obtained if we are processing a single note. If we introduce identical vibrato to three violin-like notes, the illusion of a three-piece violin section is destroyed. Similarly, if we introduce a block clarinet trill the effect isn't realistic. So you can see that a monophonic synthesizer still has an important part to play.

The Voice Module

At this stage it is worth introducing the concept of the voice module. A voice module is simply a circuit producing a single voice. It accepts three kinds of information:

1 Controller Data – concerning which note is to sound, when it is to play and for how long.

2 Performance Data – information regarding pitchbend, modulation (vibrato, trills, tremolo etc).

3 Parameter Data – concerning the setting of the individual voice elements governing pitch, timbre and loudness.

So in the above example of a simple monophonic synthesizer, we would have controller data arriving from the keyboard, performance data from the performance controls, and parameter data from the front control panel.

Polyphonic Synthesizers

There are several varieties of polyphonic synthesizer. Ideally we would envisage that a polyphonic synthesizer would have a separate voice module for every note within the span of its controller. This is known as being Fully Polyphonic. So a five octave keyboard controlled poly-synth would have 61 voice modules. Originally the very first synthesizers were fully polyphonic with separate voice

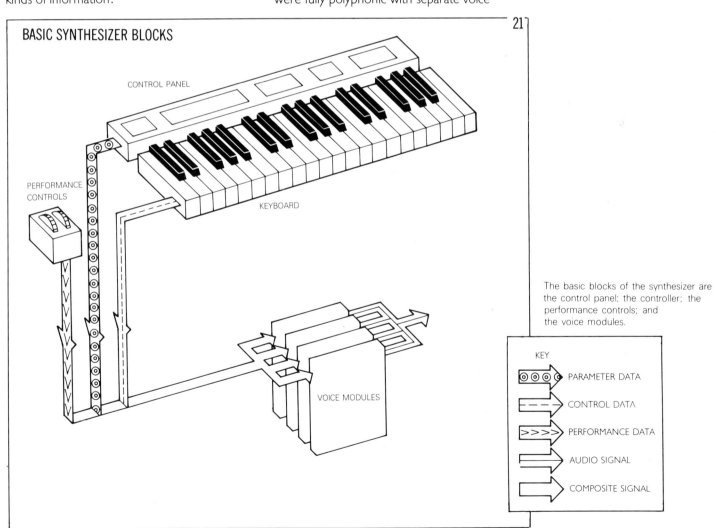

BASIC SYNTHESIZER BLOCKS

21

CONTROL PANEL

PERFORMANCE CONTROLS

KEYBOARD

VOICE MODULES

The basic blocks of the synthesizer are the control panel; the controller; the performance controls; and the voice modules.

KEY

PARAMETER DATA

CONTROL DATA

PERFORMANCE DATA

AUDIO SIGNAL

COMPOSITE SIGNAL

modules (of sorts) for each note. As you can imagine this was prohibitively expensive, and as a result the concept of the voice assignable synthesizer was evolved.

The thinking runs thus: you generally play only four to eight notes at any one time on the keyboard, so instead of having most of the voices redundant at any instant, why not have just a few moveable voices. So when you play a note, the instrument sees you are playing a certain note, then sees which voice it has free, and assigns it to that note.

The system on the whole works well. It means that you are maximising the usage of the voice-producing circuitry, and consequently keeping costs down to a minimum. There are, however, instances when this voice assignment system does have its limitations. Take an

acoustic piano, depress the sustain pedal, then play a run of notes right up the length of the keyboard. Although you may not be holding more than four or five notes at any instant, you will find that every note you've played will still be sounding as depressing the sustain pedal has removed the dampers. Thus you may have around 20-30 different 'voices' sounding simultaneously.

If you translate this to an eight voice synthesizer, you will notice that as you run up the keyboard, notes drop out as they are re-assigned to the new notes being played. So, in this instance, the voice assignable synthesizer cannot effectively handle the job. But this kind of demand on the instrument is very rare, and one that can be endured, especially when considering the savings that are made.

VOICING

TYPES OF SYNTHESIZER

3

When one is thinking of investing in an electronic music synthesizer, the overriding consideration must be the role or use to which the instrument is to be put. Buying a synthesizer is like buying a motor vehicle; you don't buy a four-wheel drive dump-truck as a family runaround. There are many different types of synthesizer; some are designed for specific tasks, others can be considered as general purpose instruments.

At this stage we aren't concerned with how the instruments actually work, we are more interested in the basic facilities the particular types of instrument offer the user. To return to our motor vehicle analogy, here we are looking at categories such as saloon, estate, hatch-back, pick-up etc; not varieties such as diesels, electric, petrol driven, etc. Although there is, necessarily, a connection between the two groups.

The range of synthesizers that are generally available fall into the following categories:

1) FULLY VARIABLES
2) PRESETS
3) PROGRAMMABLES
4) MODULARS
5) HYBRIDS
6) SAMPLERS
7) DEDICATED COMPUTERS
8) COMPUTER PERIPHERALS

The division between monophonics and polyphonics applies to all these types of instrument. So you can have a polyphonic programmable, a monophonic sampler etc. although some of these combinations are rarely encountered.

Synthesizer Building Blocks

The actual way in which the above categories of instrument work isn't of importance at this stage. But to understand the differences between the various groups, it is necessary to define the composite parts that make up a synthesizer. We can best do this by considering the synthesizer in block format then see how these groups utilise the blocks in their own different ways.

A) CENTRAL PROCESSOR
B) CONTROLLER
C) PERFORMANCE CONTROLS
D) CONTROL PANEL
E) VOICE MODULE(S)

See the system diagram, fig 22

A) The Central Processor

The heart of a synthesizer is the central processor. This is simply a series of electronic circuits that assimilate the information sent to it, and in turn sends the data to the relevant circuits. From figure 22 you can see that data is received from the control panel, the controller, and the performance controls and sent out to the voice modules.

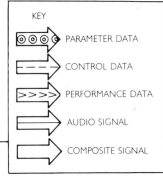

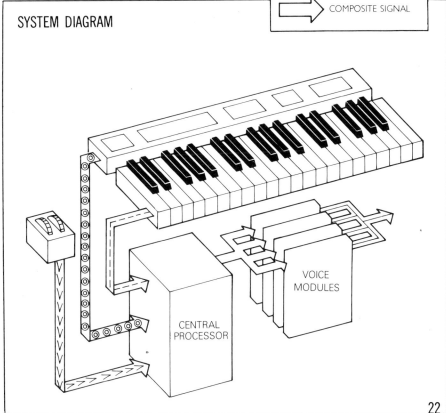

SYSTEM DIAGRAM

22

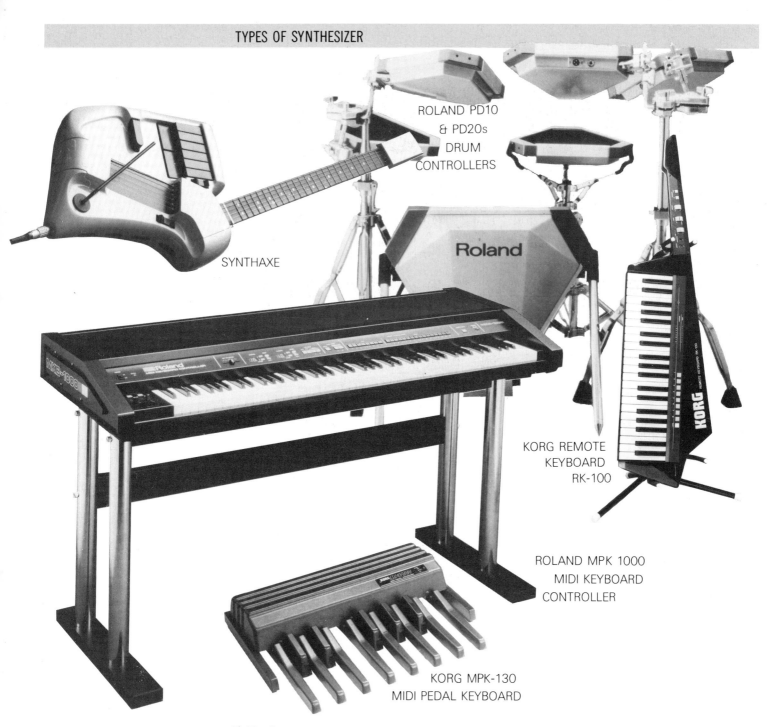

SYNTHAXE

ROLAND PD10
& PD20s
DRUM
CONTROLLERS

KORG REMOTE
KEYBOARD
RK-100

ROLAND MPK 1000
MIDI KEYBOARD
CONTROLLER

KORG MPK-130
MIDI PEDAL KEYBOARD

B) The Controller

The hardware that you actually come into physical contact with when playing the notes is known as the controller. The most common form of controller is the keyboard, but synthesizers can be driven by many different devices. Electronic guitars are fairly popular control media. There are also wind controllers, percussion controllers etc.

The controller essentially sends information as to which notes are to sound; when they are to sound; and for how long.

C) The Performance Controls

When you play a guitar you inject extra feel by perhaps bending a string momentarily to raise the pitch of a note; or when you sustain a bowed violin note you might add a degree of vibrato to enhance the sound. Well, it is possible to do this with a synthesizer, but

generally you need some extra control mechanism to introduce this kind of animation to the sound.

Remembering that a synthesizer is an instrument that lets you construct a sound from the fundamentals of pitch, timbre and loudness, the performance controls enable you to manually vary these parameters while the note is sounding.

The most commonly found performance controls are pitchbend and modulation wheels, both of which primarily affect the pitch of the sound.

More recently we have seen an increasing number of instruments featuring touch responsive keyboards. These enable the player to control other elements of the sound by striking the key at different speeds, and by applying further pressure after the note has reached its initial depressed position.

D) The Control Panel

If we are going to create our own sounds, or in fact select preset ones, we must have some buttons to push and some knobs to twiddle. That's the function of the main control panel. As well as enabling performance information to be interpreted in specific ways, the main control panel enables us to set up specific sounds and to vary the fundamental qualities of the sound.

In the early instruments, before microprocessors found their way into virtually all instruments, the controls that actually determined the settings of the various sound parameters were actually part of the voice production circuitry. Nowadays, the control panel is purely a bank of knobs and switches with no ancillary circuitry. The central processor acts as a scanning device and looks at the settings of the controls many times every second, and from this data sends the necessary signals to the voice modules.

E) The Voice Module(s)

Every synthesizer must have at least one voice module, or voice, in order to produce the sound. The voice module is the focus of all that has gone before. It is here that all the performance data (originated from the controller) and control data (originated from the control panel) ends up, and is turned into an actual signal that can then be amplified and heard. Each voice module is generally capable of producing just the one sound, therefore it naturally follows that to be able to play 'x' notes simultaneously, the synthesizer has to have at least 'x' voice modules, or voices.

These, then, are the basic constituents that make up a synthesizer. The picture isn't quite so clear cut as there are other aspects to consider, such as the input of external signals etc.

We can now return to look at the make-up of our eight basic synthesizer classifications:

1) Fully variables (FV)

The fully variable was the first commercial type of synthesizer, although its popularity has now been superseded by the Programmable (3). Figure 24 shows the basic block configuration. The FV synthesizer is more often than not a monophonic instrument. The distinguishing feature that gives it its classification is that all the various elements that can be determined when constructing a sound can be set up directly from the front panel. So the synthesizer responds directly from the settings you establish on the panel.

The main disadvantage with this kind of instrument is that you have no quick and easy way of switching from sound to sound; it takes a while to change all the settings in order to create a new sound. In the early days of the synthesizer, pro-players found it necessary to take several FV synths on stage with them, each set to a different sound, as they had no time to change settings.

EXAMPLES	: Minimoog, Moog Rogue, Roland SH-101, Yamaha CS-01, Roland Juno-6.
ADVANTAGES	: Relatively inexpensive, very versatile sound-wise.
DISADVANTAGES	: Slow to change sound.
MAIN USAGE	: Recording, budget applications.

2) Presets

The Preset Synthesizer came as a direct result of the disadvantages of the FV machines. People didn't want to spend a lot of time setting up new sounds, they simply wanted to press a switch and get, for example, an oboe sound. So, the preset instrument evolved. Usually this kind of instrument would feature a wide range of imitative sounds (mainly copies of acoustic instruments), although one or two abstract sounds were incorporated.

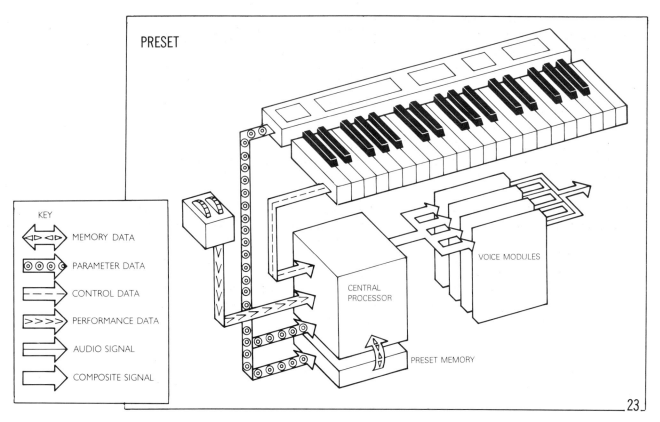

PRESET

KEY

◁▷◁▷ MEMORY DATA

⊙⊙⊙⊙ PARAMETER DATA

---▷ CONTROL DATA

>>>▷ PERFORMANCE DATA

⇨ AUDIO SIGNAL

⇨ COMPOSITE SIGNAL

VOICE MODULES

CENTRAL PROCESSOR

PRESET MEMORY

23

The main market for the preset synthesizer was with the live performer and also the home organist, who wanted a new range of sounds to add to those of his organ. As a result many preset synths were, and still are, designed to sit on top of a home organ, with the controls mounted on the front edge below the keyboard for ease of access to the seated player.

However, having gained the flexibility of being able to instantly access a particular sound, the flexibility of the instrument as a whole was diminished. Figure 23 shows the block diagram of the preset synthesizer.

The main difference here is in the central processor section, which has to call on data that has been stored in a memory bank to interpret the information sent from the control panel. If, for example, we select our oboe preset, the central processor sees that button has been depressed on the control panel, and then has to send some information to the voice modules in order that they may set themselves up to produce the desired sound. This information is stored in a preset memory bank. So upon selecting our oboe voicing the processor looks into the memory to find how that sound is constructed and simply feeds that data to the voice modules.

EXAMPLES	: Roland Promars, Kawai 100-P, Korg Sigma.
ADVANTAGES	: Fast to use.
DISADVANTAGES	: You are restricted to preset sounds.
MAIN USAGE	: Live, as a home organ add-on.

3) Programmables

The natural evolution, incorporating the versatility of the FV synth with the speed of operation of the Preset, would be to design a synthesizer in which you could 'construct' your

THE OSCAR

own preset sounds. And with the advances in digital technology, the means to do this became realisable. In fact the first programmable instruments were polyphonic, and they appeared around the late 1970s.

Figure 24 shows the similarities between the Preset and the Programmable machines. Here, instead of having a fixed memory bank from which to recall preset control data, the memory is now alterable. So the passage of data is both to and from the memory.

In addition, the control panel is far busier as it combines all the knobs and switches of the FV machines with the selector buttons of the preset instrument.

When you 'create' one of your own sounds, the controls of the front panel are set to provide the desired effect. The processor then scans all the controls and stores settings in a designated part of the memory. Upon the selection of that memory location using the selector switches, the processor sends the stored information to the voice modules, not the data depicted by the then current settings of the control panel.

There are now both polyphonic and monophonic programmable synthesizers, and these are by far and away the most prominent variety of instrument. They are naturally enough equally suited to both live and studio work. Not surprisingly a programmable instrument is generally more expensive than an FV or Preset synthesizer, but more recently the price difference between the two has narrowed considerably.

EXAMPLES   : Roland Juno-106, Sequential Circuits
                  Prophet 5, OSCar, PPG Wave 2.3,
                  "Yamaha DX-5, DX-7, and DX-21"
ADVANTAGES   : Fast to use, versatile.
DISADVANTAGES   : Slightly more expensive.
MAIN USAGE   : Live.

4) Modulars

In the early days of synthesis, electronic design boffins concentrated on building modular systems. A modular system, naturally enough, is one that consists of a series of modules, which would be patched together using audio cables to produce a configuration that would enable the user to attain the desired effect. Now, of course, MIDI offers even more possibilities

So a modular synthesizer might consist of 6 oscillator modules, a variety of filter modules, envelope shapers, amplifiers, inverters, lag generators etc. A controller such as a keyboard is used to provide performance and controller data. The beauty of this system is its immense flexibility. For example, you could have the system so arranged that a keyboard controller sets the pitches of all the oscillators, then routes half of them to one kind of filter; the others might be sent to some form of reverberation unit, then all signals would be mixed together, further filtered, and shaped. There are an infinite number of possibilities.

A modular system generally utilises a monophonic controller, but being primarily a studio device this presents few problems as composite tracks can be multi-layered.

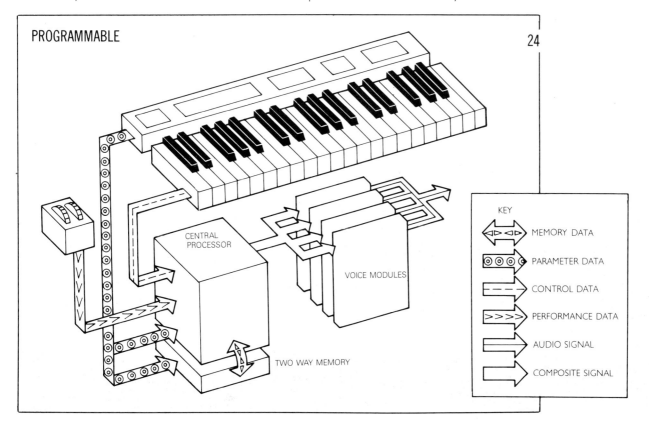

PROGRAMMABLE   24

CENTRAL PROCESSOR

VOICE MODULES

TWO WAY MEMORY

KEY

MEMORY DATA

PARAMETER DATA

CONTROL DATA

PERFORMANCE DATA

AUDIO SIGNAL

COMPOSITE SIGNAL

THE MOOG OPUS 3

EXAMPLES : Moog Series III, Roland 100M System, Serge Modular.
ADVANTAGES : Incredibly versatile.
DISADVANTAGES: Expensive and slow to set up.
MAIN USAGE : Studio.

5) Hybrids

There are several different kinds of hybrid synthesizer, but the most popular is the so-called Sandwich Synthesizer (figure 25.).

Strictly speaking the Sandwich-Synth isn't a true synthesizer; it often owes quite a bit more to organ technology than to synthesis techniques. Usually it consists of an electronic organ section, a string synthesizer section, and a pseudo-polyphonic synth section.

When you press a note on the keyboard, the various sections are all triggered and told by the central processor to sound that note. So in terms of creating textured, layered sounds the sandwich-synth excels, but for truly creative synthesis work this type of instrument is not particularly suitable. All sandwich synths are polyphonic.

Another hybrid is the Vocoder (figure 26.) which evolved from voice scrambling techniques used in World War II. Essentially, a vocoder is a device that imparts the animation of one sound on to another. So if, for example, you took the sound of a waterfall, you could give it the characteristics of a human voice, and effectively make the waterfall talk.

EXAMPLES : Korg Trident (sandwich), Roland VP-330 (vocoder). Moog OPUS 3
ADVANTAGES : Unique characteristics.
DISADVANTAGES: Relatively limited in scope. Expensive.
MAIN USAGE : Studio and effects.

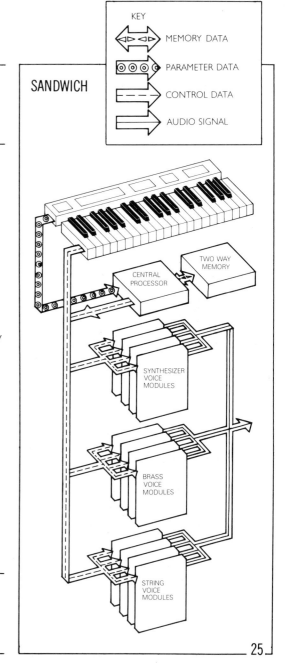

SANDWICH

KEY

◁▷ ◁▷ MEMORY DATA

◎◎◎ PARAMETER DATA

- - - → CONTROL DATA

⇨ AUDIO SIGNAL

25

6) Samplers

Probably the most logical way to be able to get the desired sound from an instrument and to use it musically is to actually make a recording of a real sound, then manipulate it until you achieve the desired effect. This process is known as sampling. (Figure 27).

Quite simply you make a recording of any sound – say a car horn hooting – then you feed this into a "Sampling Synthesizer". This turns the sound into a series of numbers which the central processor can manipulate and send the characteristics of that sound to the individual voice modules. The controller then triggers these voices and they in turn re-create the sample at the pitch of the assinged note.

The sampling keyboard is probably one of the most exciting new areas of electronic music synthesis, but in the strictest sense of the term, it really isn't synthesis at all.

There are also instruments that incorporate factory loaded samples which can be changed only by inserting new memory chips (circuits). These are usually less expensive, but of course they are far less versatile.

EXAMPLES	: Emulator II, Simmons SDS-EPB Ensoniq Mirage
ADVANTAGES	: Unlimited range of sounds.
DISADVANTAGES:	Duration of sample. Expensive.
MAIN USAGE	: Studio and live.

7) Dedicated Computers

Most electronic music synthesizers incorporate some form of microprocessor system, i.e. a small internal computer handles all the information processing. But there are also special computers designed specifically for musical applications. These are generally based on a mainframe computer that has been modified to handle the vast amounts of data

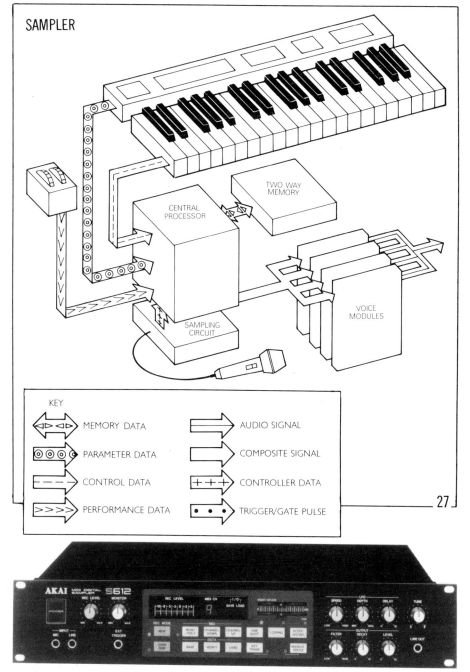

SAMPLER

KEY

⬄ MEMORY DATA   ⬜➡ AUDIO SIGNAL

◎◎◎ PARAMETER DATA   ⬜➡ COMPOSITE SIGNAL

--➡ CONTROL DATA   +++➡ CONTROLLER DATA

>>>> PERFORMANCE DATA   •••➡ TRIGGER/GATE PULSE

27

AKAI S612 DIGITAL SAMPLER

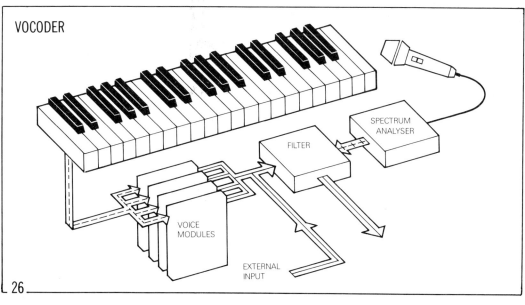

VOCODER

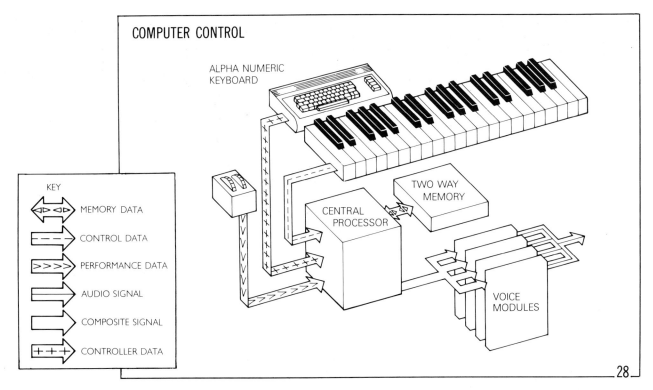

COMPUTER CONTROL

ALPHA NUMERIC KEYBOARD

TWO WAY MEMORY

CENTRAL PROCESSOR

VOICE MODULES

KEY

MEMORY DATA

CONTROL DATA

PERFORMANCE DATA

AUDIO SIGNAL

COMPOSITE SIGNAL

CONTROLLER DATA

28

processing such high performance devices dictate.

One of the most useful aspects of this kind of instrument is the opportunity to visualise all the sound creation processors on a VDU (visual display monitor). As can be seen from figure 28 the basic configuration of this system does not vary dramatically from that of the conventional programmable polyphonic synthesizer. However, the actual performance characteristics are considerably more advanced.

EXAMPLES	: Fairlight CMI, Synclavier II.
ADVANTAGES	: Versatile, easy to use (relatively speaking).
DISADVANTAGES	: Very expensive.
MAIN USAGE	: Studio, in particular film and television work.

8) Computer Peripherals

This form of synthesizer is generally not of the real time variety; that is to say you cannot use the instrument for performance. Here a personal or home computer takes the place of the controller, central processor and control panel, and the ensuing data is fed to a series of voice modules to effect the desired result.

So the actual system would consist of a home computer with voice modules as the peripherals. Then all that is needed is the relevant software (computer program) that tells the computer's processor what data to feed to the voice modules. Note and sound data is entered *via* the computer's alpha-numeric keyboard.

In some instances proper chromatic keyboards have been designed to integrate into such systems. Thus the voices can be played in

real time (i.e. live), rather than telling the computer to play a certain note for a certain time then another one etc.

Another form of such peripheral is the Computer-to-MIDI interface, which enables the computer to talk to standard types of synthesizer.

To the serious musician a computer with musical peripherals is of most use as a compositional aid. With most such devices the computer enables the user to build up note by note and track by track his complete score, then to synchronise the music to other instruments such as a rhythm unit.

Originally these peripherals were primarily designed to give computer enthusiasts an insight into the world of music, enabling them to turn a computer into a musical production facility. But more recently, with the advent of such systems as Yamaha's CX-5M, far more professional results have been attainable.

Here a standard home computer has been modified with the express aim of providing a central core to a budget electronic music studio. And because the computer isn't dedicated to one specific task, reprogramming enables it to be used not only to create new sounds, and as a compositional aid, but also to coordinate pictures with sound. Thus you have a simple audio-visual production facility. More on Computer Peripheral Synthesis later.

EXAMPLES	: SCI/Commodore 64 MIDI Sequencer, Yamaha CX-5M, Acorn AMPLE, alphaSyntauri.
ADVANTAGES	: Low cost, very flexible.
DISADVANTAGES	: Not suitable for live work.
MAIN USAGE	: Home, studios.

SUBTRACTIVE SYNTHESIS 4

In this chapter we look at how synthesizers work, i.e. what each knob and switch does and why. Unfortunately, as with the types of synthesizer, the subject fragments into various different technologies, all of which are important if you want to understand when and how to use a certain kind of synthesizer.

This chapter deals primarily with the workings of the voice module, or modules, as introduced in the previous chapter. These generally function in one of the following conventions:

1) SUBTRACTIVE SYNTHESIS
2) ADDITIVE (HARMONIC) SYNTHESIS
3) FM ALGORITHMIC SYNTHESIS
4) PHASE DISTORTION SYNTHESIS
5) GEOMETRIC SYNTHESIS
6) DIRECT SYNTHESIS
7) CONSONANT/VOWEL SYNTHESIS
8) PLUCKED STRING SYNTHESIS

Quite a checklist, and although many of you may be familiar with some of these types of synthesis, few will be familiar with all varieties.

There are several reasons for the prominence of such a wide range of synthesis techniques. Primarily the different systems offer the end user a different 'quality' of sound and allow freedom to explore different tonal directions. But manufacturers have always tried to open up new avenues in order to ensure a) they have a bigger share of the market than their competitors, and b) that the whole market doesn't stagnate.

There are other reasons. Technology has enabled us to perform tasks that just a few years ago seemed both practically and economically impossible. Five years ago a synthesis technique that might have promised the moon and stars would have seemed far too expensive to be workable, but with certain electronic production advancements, such a technique is now quite feasible.

And, of course, patent law is a stumbling block to companies wishing to follow certain synthesis paths. One company may hold the patent for a complete system of creating sounds. A competitor is, therefore, unable to bring out instruments utilising those methods, and has to commit vast sums developing

another approach.

On the whole all this leads to the instrument buying public getting a wider choice of competitively priced instruments reflecting the state of the technology of the day.

The only problem is . . . how does it all work ?

Voltage Control

Synthesis is all about control.

It was the advent of the transistor in the Fifties that created the environment for the development of voltage control. And it is thanks to the pioneering work of electronic inventors such as Bob Moog, Alan Pearlman and Herb Deutch, that the musical possibilities of using voltages to control sound were realised. Synthesis relies on the definition of the three parameters, pitch, timbre, and loudness, to create the desired sound.

Take for example the element pitch. You have high notes and low notes. If you could specify the pitch by means of a voltage you would have an extremely workable system. Similarly if you expressed the other parameters using just voltages then you would have the basis of a sound synthesizer system.

To create a specific sound, all three elements need to be able to vary over the duration of the note, so the control voltage will have to be able to vary accordingly. However, we need other circuits that can produce voltages which change as we want them to.

Again consider the element of pitch. We've seen that a pitch is produced by an oscillating medium creating a compression and rarefaction in the air pressure. We need a voltage controlled oscillator that operates so that as the voltage increases, so does the pitch. Simple ? Well actually it wasn't as simple a development as it might appear. For one reason, it is important that every voltage controlled oscillator functions in exactly the same way as the next one. If it doesn't there are serious tuning problems. This was one of the major problems of the early voltage controlled instruments.

The voltage controlled circuits of the synthesizer operate (usually) from low level low power voltages between zero and 15 volts.

It should be understood that there is a

difference between the voltages that are used to control elements and the actual electricity used to make the circuits work. These are of the same order of magnitude, but fixed.

It should also be understood that if, for example, a voltage controlled oscillator is receiving a control voltage of maybe 10 volts and hence running faster than if it were being fed a 5 volt signal, it is not drawing more power from the control signal. The control voltage is purely an instruction. It does no actual work in causing the circuit to oscillate faster.

The Oberheim 8 voice synthesizer uses a 1v per octave scaling system and is now something of an anachronism.

Controllers

Before launching into the various techniques of synthesizing sound, let's start with the part of the synthesizer through which the musician communicates his musical talents – the controller.

Undoubtedly the most common form of controller is the keyboard. There is no reason why other devices cannot be used, for the time being we shall be considering just the keyboard as the control medium.

The role of the controller is to supply the voice modules with data specifying:

1 Which notes are to sound
2 When each note is to begin
3 When each note is to end

Controller data (analogue)

In the early days of synthesizer technology, voltages would be derived straight from the keyboard. There would be a voltage chain running down the keyboard, and the higher the note played the greater the voltage produced.

You will notice from the diagram that for every octave span of the keyboard the voltage produced rises by one volt – the "one volt per octave" convention. This has become a universal standard for most such synthesizers, and is known as a logarithmic relationship.

Why ? Because as we've seen pitch is a non-linear phenomenon. The frequency between the note 'A' oscillating at 440 Hz ('A-440') and the 'A' an octave below (220 Hz) is 220Hz; however, the frequency gap between 'A-440' and the 'A' an octave above (880 Hz) is 440Hz. So we have a frequency to pitch and voltage relationship as illustrated in figure 29. Thus an increase of 1/12 volt (a semitone) at the bottom end of the keyboard necessitates a change of frequency that is far less than that produced by a 1/12 volt change towards the top end of the keyboard.

Unfortunately, the "one volt per octave" standardization was not adhered to by all manufacturers. Some preferred to adopt a linear scaling whereby the frequency rises by 1000Hz (say) for every volt rise in the control voltage. In this instance the control voltage output from the keyboard would be as shown in figure 31.

This direct generation of a voltage from the keyboard also requires some method of stipulating when each note begins and ends (ii and iii). So another set of keyboard contacts had to be employed to produce what is known as a gate pulse.

Figure 30 illustrates the way in which a gate

1v PER OCTAVE SCALING
29

2093 Hz

1046.5 Hz

261.62Hz

130.81 Hz

0v   1v   2v   3v   4v   5v

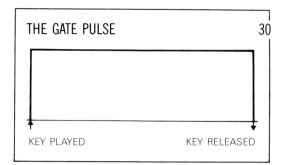

KEY PLAYED   KEY RELEASED

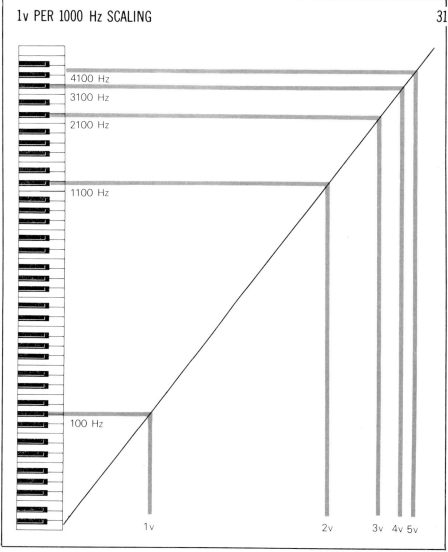

pulse operates. The pulse is simply a fixed voltage that is presented to every note of the keyboard. When a key is pressed this pulse is triggered, and it remains ON until the key is released. Not all instruments utilised the same type of gate pulse. Consequently, as with the voltage control convention, not all instruments could be linked to one another.

The real problems with this kind of analogue system came when a polyphonic controller was needed. Here it is relatively easy to get a control voltage from a keyboard and a simultaneous gate pulse in the circuit.

But to extract the several voltages required to produce a chord, and then to be able to ensure that the gate pulses matched up to the chords being played, was a far more complex problem for the analogue circuit designers, and in the end it was felt necessary to opt for a digital system.

Controller data (digital)

The use of the microprocessor to handle all the information makes things considerably easier. Instead of having to produce separate note and timing data, all can now be produced from a single signal. Polyphony too is no longer a problem.

How ? As with all digital systems the answer is to consider tiny packages of time, then put them all together so that they form a continuous chain of events. Every note of the keyboard is scanned (looked at sequentially) by the central processor. If a key is being played, then the central processor notes this fact and acts upon it. Any key can be only on or off so this is an ideal digital situation. When the processor has looked at all the notes, it cycles back to the beginning and repeats the process.

This is all done at very high speed: every key is 'scanned' at least 50 times a second. The beauty of this system is that we are purely manipulating numbers, and the time scale is fixed – there is no need to have a separate trigger pulse as the processor knows (to the nearest 1/50th second) exactly when each key has been played.

Voice Assignment

What happens to the information as it is assimilated by the central processor ?

In a monophonic instrument, the processor simply translates the controller data into language that the voice module will understand, i.e. pitch and timing data, and transmits it virtually instantaneously. This seems straightforward enough, but what happens if two notes are played simultaneously ? Or if one is held and another subsequently played ?

Various conventions exist:

1 High Note Priority, where the highest note being played on the keyboard is assigned to the voice module.
2 Low Note Priority, where the lowest note being played on the keyboard is assigned to the voice module.
3 Last Note Priority, where the last note to be played on the keyboard, even if others are being held, is assigned to the voice module.

LAST NOTE PRIORITY
1 Note 'C' is played and held and thus assigned to Voice 1
2 Notes 'E', 'F' and 'G' are subsequently played and held, and consequently assigned to Voices 2, 3, and 4.
3 Note 'B' is subsequently played, and Voice 1 is re-assigned from 'C' to the new 'B', even though 'C' continues to be held.

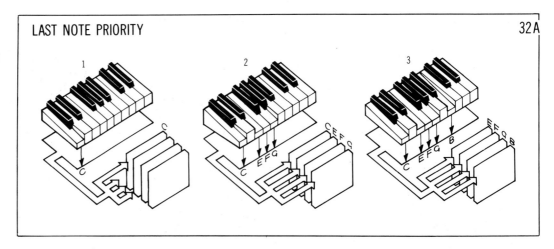

LAST NOTE PRIORITY 32A

HELD NOTE PRIORITY
1 Notes 'C', 'E', 'F' and 'G' are played and held. They are assigned to Voices 1 to 4.
2 Note 'B' is subsequently played and held, but because all notes are being held there is no Voice available, consequently the 'B' does not sound.
3 Only when a note F is released does a voice become free, and thus the 'B' (which is still being held) can sound.

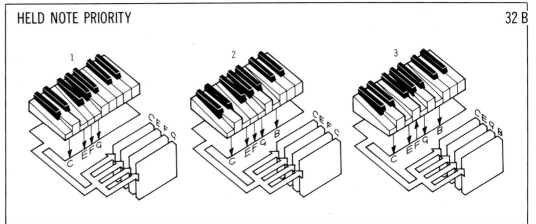

HELD NOTE PRIORITY 32 B

The priority systems are important as each is suited to a particular playing style.

With a polyphonic system there is an additional problem, as to which voice module the processor sends the information.

Say we have a six-voice polyphonic synthesizer. There are many different ways in which the controller data can be assigned to the individual voice. The first note played can be assigned to Voice No.1. Every new note played can be assigned to the next free voice, i.e. one that isn't sounding etc. But, what happens if seven notes are being played simultaneously ? You can use only six at any given instant.

In the early days several different polyphonic assignment modes existed. But over the years just two have prevailed.

1 Last note priority.
2 Held note priority.

Both utilise a 'queueing' system. When the keyboard is in use all voices not assigned a note queue up to be given a note. As a key is released the voice that has been assigned to that note goes to the back of the queue to await a new assignment. So we have a situation as depicted by figure 32.

The above two priority cases come into play only when more keys than there are voices are being held down. Then, the last note priority mode causes the voice that has been held the longest to be reassigned to the newly played key, and consequently that first note disappears. In held note priority mode no new note is assigned a voice until one of the other keys has been released, thus freeing a voice.

This assignment code may seem something of an obscure subject at this stage, but you will find it a most important consideration sometimes. Especially if you are using your polyphonic synthesizer for simultaneous lead line and accompaniment work. If the instruments were of the held note priority version, you might find that parts of your melody fail to turn up as all the voices have been assigned to the accompaniment. Similarly, the use of the last note priority system might mean that you abruptly lose an important element of a sustained chord. It's a clear case of horses for courses.

There are other aspects relating to the controller in the world of synthesis and these are dealt with more fully in chapter 8.

Subtractive Synthesis

Subtractive Synthesis is based on the concept that you start with a sound of the desired pitch, which is rich in harmonics, and you derive the sound you require by removing all the unwanted harmonics. The concept of subtractive synthesis enabled the synthesizer that we know today to evolve over the past couple of decades, thanks to the advent of voltage control.

Voice Module (subtractive)

Figure 33 shows in block diagram format a simple subtractive synthesizer voice module. Remember that there are three types of signal input: controller data, originating from the keyboard or whatever control medium is employed; performance data, from the performance controls (pitchbender, touch keyboard etc.); and parameter data, determining the actual quality of the sound that is to be produced. For the moment we will ignore performance data.

The subtractive synthesizer's voice module generally features two voltage controlled oscillators per voice along with a noise source. The latter is a device that produces a random mixture of all frequencies in the audio spectrum – very useful in subtractive synthesis.

These are then mixed to form a composite 'audio' signal, thus the element of pitch has been taken care of. Here the term 'audio' refers to an electronic representation of an audio waveform, as distinct from a control voltage signal.

The audio output from the mixer is then fed into the voltage controlled filter. The filter removes unwanted harmonics, resulting in a sound with the desired timbre. The amount and degree of filtering is, naturally enough, voltage controlled.

The third and final stage is to set the loudness of the sound, so the audio signal (still, of course, in electrical format) is then fed through a voltage controlled amplifier. This simply adjusts the amplitude of the signal in direct response to the control voltage fed to it.

Now this seems simple enough, but so far we've failed to take account of the dynamic changes: as the note sounds, all these three parameters need to change. If this were not the case, and we'd applied a constant voltage to the VCA, there would be no change in the output level of the sound and the note would drone on for ever.

The circuits that are used to make these continual changes are known as modifiers, and there are two main varieties – envelope generators and low frequency oscillators. In the

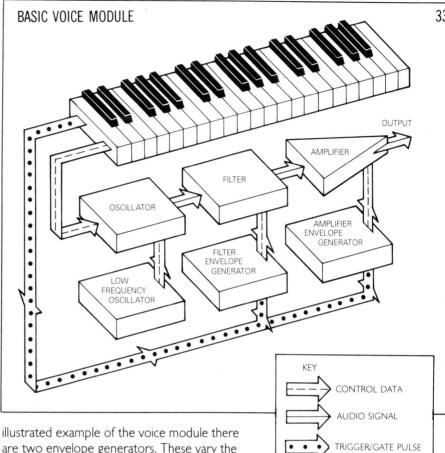

OUTPUT

AMPLIFIER

FILTER

OSCILLATOR

AMPLIFIER ENVELOPE GENERATOR

FILTER ENVELOPE GENERATOR

LOW FREQUENCY OSCILLATOR

KEY
CONTROL DATA
AUDIO SIGNAL
TRIGGER/GATE PULSE

illustrated example of the voice module there are two envelope generators. These vary the amplitude and timbre over the course of the sound, and the low frequency oscillator is generally used to vary the pitch of the note, thus producing vibrato and trill effects.

The output from the voltage controlled amplifier marks the end of the chain, and if it is a polyphonic instrument this signal can then be mixed with the outputs from the other voice modules and taken to an external amplifier and speakers.

When considering the subtractive synthesizer two alternative oscillator systems can be employed – the voltage controlled oscillator (VCO) and the digitally controlled oscillator (DCO). What's the difference ?

The Voltage Controlled Oscillator (VCO)

The VCO is considered to be part of each voice module. As can be seen from figure 34, it receives control voltages from:

A the controller (*via* the processor) telling it the pitch of the note to be played.
B the front panel controls (*via* the processor) which set the tuning bias of the oscillator.
C the low frequency oscillator (from the voice module, but in amount controlled by the processor) for possible modulation.
D the performance controls (*via* the processor) for pitchbend effects etc.
E a possible external source for sequencing effects etc.

OSCILLATOR INPUTS

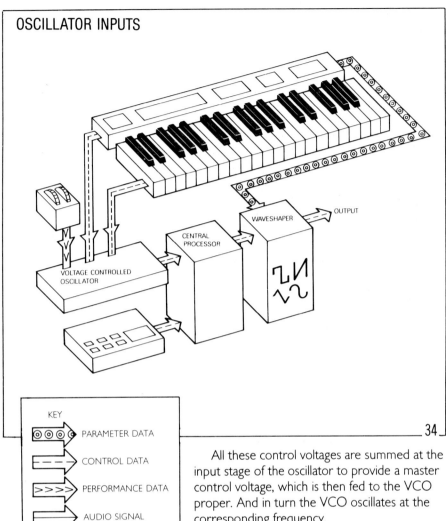

KEY

⊚⊚⊚⊚▷ PARAMETER DATA

├ ─ ─ ▷ CONTROL DATA

▷ ▷ ▷ ▷ PERFORMANCE DATA

⟹ AUDIO SIGNAL

_34_

can see, any tuning problem is overcome by the digital pitch generation stage. This is a somewhat simplified vision of the DCO, as, of course, provision does have to be made to feed modulation data from the voice module back to the central processor in order to effect vibrato, trills etc.

Phase

The purity and mathematical precision of a waveform derived from a VCO or DCO gives it a rather cold, unnatural feel. So in order to get over this problem, many synthesizers utilising subtractive techniques employ more than one oscillator per voice. The result is a much more natural, fuller sound, and a more flexible instrument.

Consider the difference in tonal characteristics between a six-string and twelve-string guitar. The strings are arranged so that every time a note is played, two strings tuned in unison sound, not just the one. The result is a much warmer, rounded sound. An acoustic piano also has more than one sound generator per note – i.e. most keys activate a hammer that simultaneously strikes two or three strings tuned to the same pitch, and this again gives the instrument a fuller sound – why is this ?

Consider two oscillators producing triangle waveforms at exactly the same pitch (see figure 35). The chances are that they won't start at exactly the same time. That is to say one will reach a peak before the other. Now, if we add the two of these waveforms together we get a new waveform, which isn't simply a triangle wave of twice the proportions. You can see from the diagram that the top section of the waveform has flattened out. This is because one waveform is still rising while the other is falling, and as they are doing this at the same rate they cancel one another out.

In figure 35 the two waveforms are said to be out of phase with one another.

Figure 36 shows other examples of what happens when the phase difference varies. Note that phase cancellation can occur if the waveforms are exactly one half cycle out of phase with one another – then there is no resultant waveform.

As things stand we are simply producing a new static waveform from the two others that are perfectly in tune with one another. But now look what happens if we slightly detune one of the oscillators. (Figure 37). In order to make the diagram of manageable dimensions, let's look at what happens when a triangle wave of ten cycles per second is mixed with one of eleven.

Because the frequencies are not exactly the same, the phase difference between the two waveforms is constantly changing, and as a

All these control voltages are summed at the input stage of the oscillator to provide a master control voltage, which is then fed to the VCO proper. And in turn the VCO oscillates at the corresponding frequency.

Because of the internal circuit structure of a VCO it is possible to take feeds from various parts of the circuitry, such that different waveshapes are produced.

A basic VCO will generate sawtooth and square waveforms. However, if other waveforms such as triangle, pulse, or sine, are required further waveshaping is necessary.

The Digitally Controlled Oscillator (DCO)

This is a more recent development brought about a) by the bad press analogue VCOs were receiving regarding their inability to hold their tuning, and b) because the pitch could be directly generated by the central processor.

The parameter data determines the basic starting pitch of the oscillators, and the performance and controller data set the actual note to be played. So, as all of this data is fed into the central processor, it is possible for it, and a few other bits of circuitry, to output a train of pulses at a frequency that corresponds to the desired pitch. The only 'oscillator' circuitry that forms part of the voice module as such is a waveshaper.

The waveshaper takes the raw train of pulses, and translates them into the desired waveforms – square, sawtooth etc. So as you

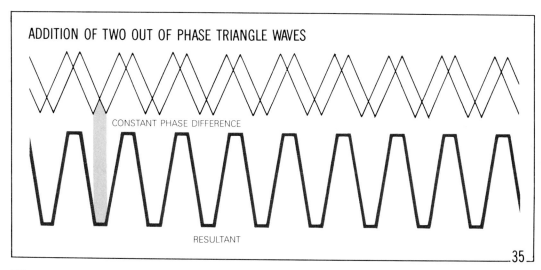

ADDITION OF TWO OUT OF PHASE TRIANGLE WAVES

CONSTANT PHASE DIFFERENCE

RESULTANT

35

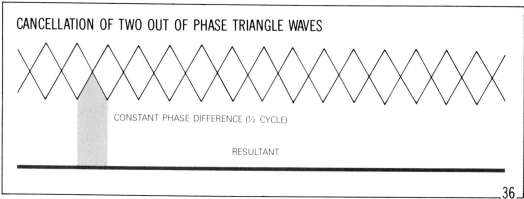

CANCELLATION OF TWO OUT OF PHASE TRIANGLE WAVES

CONSTANT PHASE DIFFERENCE (½ CYCLE)

RESULTANT

36

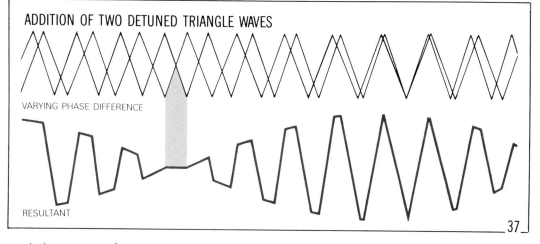

ADDITION OF TWO DETUNED TRIANGLE WAVES

VARYING PHASE DIFFERENCE

RESULTANT

37

result the new waveform consists of a series of different triangle-like waveforms of varying amplitudes. Note that the new waveform repeats itself once every second, although it will have an apparent pitch of 10.5Hz.

If we were to consider waveforms of 440Hz and 441Hz, we would still find that the pattern repeated itself once every second (441-440=1), that the sound would have an apparent pitch of 440.5Hz, and that it would also appear to decrease and increase in volume once a second.

This is known as the beating effect, and for two oscillators with frequencies in close proximity to one another, the beat frequency is the difference between the two initial frequencies.

The enhancement of the tonal quality of a sound produced by this beating effect is far greater than one would possibly expect. But if you set the frequencies of the two oscillators more than seven or eight cyles per second apart, the human ear can detect two distinct sounds. These will jar and sound very out of tune.

The concept of the beat frequency is equally applicable to acoustic sounds as well as electronic, and is one that has been used throughout the ages to tune instruments. By eliminating any beat frequency you can ensure that an instrument is producing exactly the same note as that of a reference tone (a tuning fork perhaps).

MULTI-OSCILLATOR VOICING

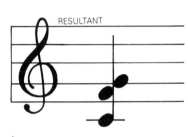

38

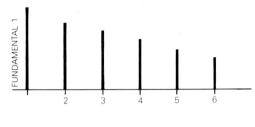

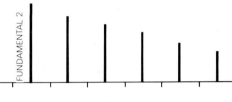

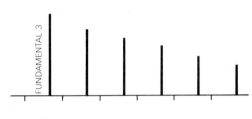

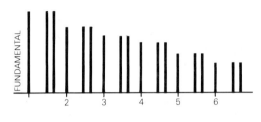

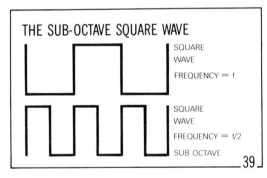

▲
If three oscillators are set to produce a root, 4th and 5th intervals, the playing of a single note will sound a complete chord. The corresponding harmonic structures that make up the chord are shown above.

THE SUB-OCTAVE SQUARE WAVE

SQUARE WAVE
FREQUENCY = f

SQUARE WAVE
FREQUENCY = f/2
SUB OCTAVE
39

Multi-Oscillator Voice Modules

The increase in 'quality' isn't the only advantage to be gained from having more than one oscillator per voice. In a dual oscillator configuration, the two oscillators need not be tuned to the same note, they can be tuned at any interval apart, an octave, a fifth, an octave and a fifth, etc. This vastly enhances the possible harmonic content of the raw sound before it is processed by the filter. Which is exactly what you need to be able to do in subtractive synthesis. In a three oscillator per voice instrument (such as the Minimoog) things are taken even further. Say all three oscillators are set to produce sawtooth waveforms, pitched so that the interval between VCOs (or DCOs if

relevant) 1 and 2 is a fourth, and VCOs 1 and 3 a fifth. Thus, with reference to figure 38, if you played the note 'C' on the keyboard VCO 1 would play a 'C', VCO 2 would play an 'F', and VCO 3 a 'G'. This gives rise to the harmonic spectrum shown in figure 38 which presents the filter with a full set of harmonics on which to work. Incidentally, this oscillator 'voicing' was extremely effectively utilised by Keith Emerson on ELP's "Tarkus" album as the solo theme to the title track.

Another useful facility of the 2- or 3- oscillator voice is the splitting of the oscillator to provide the "raw-source" from oscillators several octaves apart. This enables the filter to be used as a dynamic volume control for either the higher or lower frequencies of the composite signal .

Obviously a price has to be paid for having more than one oscillator per voice. And that price is simply a financial one. Instruments featuring single oscillator voice modules are most definitely cheaper, but then they don't offer the range of sound production facilities.

The Single Oscillator Voice Module

A single waveform emanating from a VCO or DCO is not, to say the least, the most exciting of sounds. Its timbral quality can be enhanced by filtering, and if possible various spatial effects (chorusing, phasing, echo, reverb etc.), but manufacturers have come up with other ideas to enhance the performance of such instruments.

The Sub Octave Derivative
This facility takes the raw pitch of a VCO or DCO and divides it by two or four to produce a pitch exactly one or two octaves below that of the oscillator. This pitch is then generally transformed into a square wave, as this has a greater dominance of the fundamental (1st harmonic), as well as a smoother and more rounded timbre. The sub-octave oscillation is mixed with the original pitch to produce a composite waveform rich in harmonics and powerful in content.

It should be noted that the sub-octave waveform is derived directly from the oscillator's output, and therefore there is no phase angle or phase movement between the two signals. Figure 39 shows this more clearly. The sub-octave oscillation facility is an extremely useful facet of a synthesizer, and one that is surprisingly inexpensive for manufacturers to incorporate in the design of their instruments.

Pulse Width Modulation (PWM)
This phenomenon is an extremely important

one, not only with respect to the single oscillator voice module, but also in more advanced subject areas such as digital recordings of real sounds.

If used correctly, the effect that PWM can bring to a single oscillator is surprisingly similar to that obtained when beating two oscillators against one another.

Pulse width modulation is the periodic (repeated in a constant manner) change of the duty cycle of a pulse wave (duty cycle – see p.15). Usually the modulating source is the low frequency oscillator's sine or triangle wave. A smoothly undulating waveform is necessary in order to modulate the waveform as any sudden change in level (as from a square or sawtooth waveform) would destroy the effect.

Pulse width modulation is in this instance a voltage controlled effect. The low frequency oscillator's sine wave (say) provides a voltage level that oscillates about the zero volt mean, as shown in figure 40. As the waveform rises, so the ratio between the upper and lower periods of the waveform decreases, i.e. the waveform spends most of its time at a low level (duty cycle 10% say – 10:90). As the modulating waveform's voltage passes through the zero volts level, its effect becomes negligible and the oscillator puts out a symmetrical square wave (DC=50% – 50:50). And, naturally enough, as the LFO dips into a negative value, so the duty cycle responds to produce a waveform that spends most of its time 'high' (DC-90%, 90:10.) This is clearly shown in the diagram.

Note that the actual pitch of the carrier waveform never changes. The time taken up by one cycle remains constant. Pulse width modulation is about ratios, not absolutes. It is also the case that a pulse waveform of 10% duty cycle has the same harmonic make-up as one with a 90% duty cycle. This makes sense, because one is purely a mirror image of the other across the horizontal axis.

If you were to listen to a PWM'd waveform of (say) 440Hz being modulated by a 1Hz LFO, the result would sound very similar to that of a 440Hz square wave superimposed on a 441Hz square wave of similar magnitude. These two waveforms are depicted graphically in figure 41. Again, for reasons of scale, 10Hz and 11Hz waveforms are used, but the results are equally relevant. The waveforms may not actually look that similar, the latter being distorted by the centre line. But you will notice that the actual pulse width of the composite from the mixed waveforms is changing in a very similar manner to that of the PWM'd waveform.

The pulse width modulation facility is a useful one, as shown, but it cannot replace the flexibility of having two oscillators.

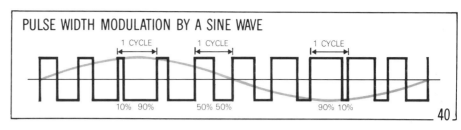

PULSE WIDTH MODULATION BY A SINE WAVE

1 CYCLE   1 CYCLE   1 CYCLE

10% 90%   50% 50%   90% 10%

40

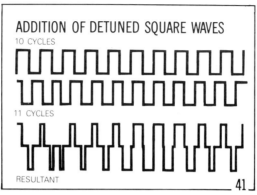

ADDITION OF DETUNED SQUARE WAVES

10 CYCLES

11 CYCLES

RESULTANT

41

Noise

When you listen to a quiet passage of music on a tape recorder you can usually hear a rather annoying constant background hiss. This is an example of noise. Here it is unwanted, and electronic design engineers strive to eliminate its effects as much as possible. But in the subtractive electronic music synthesizer, there is actually a circuit designed to produce noise as it is a valuable signal source with which to work.

Noise, as mentioned in a later chapter, is an unpitched sound source made up of random combinations of all the frequencies of the audio spectrum. The acoustic manifestation of a noise signal is a constant hissing sound. Figure 42 shows graphically how the noise source incorporates all the frequencies across the audio spectrum. Figure 42a is taken as a freeze-frame representation depicting an instant in time, while figure 42b shows an average taken over a period of time.

Because noise is a random combination of harmonics and doesn't repeat itself, it therefore has no vestige of pitch. If a waveform constantly repeats itself, it has a pitch of frequency determined by how often it repeats itself. Noise never repeats itself, it is an aperiodic waveform, and thus, in its perfect form, gives no trace of pitch.

Noise is a fantastic tool in subtractive synthesis where you generally need to start with a tone composed of many harmonics then remove the elements of the sound you don't require. However, the dexterity of the 'removal' circuitry will never be sufficient to get away from some kind of hissing sound; it is possible, however, to use the noise source either as a part of a pitched sound, e.g. the

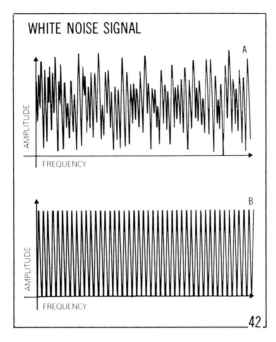

WHITE NOISE SIGNAL

42

breathy *chiff* during the attack phase of an overblown flute voicing, or to actually remove and enhance such frequencies so as to give the noise source a recognisable pitch (see filtering noise p.47).

As noise is a random collection of frequencies, there is no actual input to the sound production circuit required – i.e. you can't control noise. Having said that, there are various types of noise signal. These result from playing with the "randomness" of the sound, i.e. there's random noise and there's organized random noise.

It is at this point that we should introduce the concept of "coloured" noise, illustrated with respect to the optical analogy.

In the same way in which white light is made

up of combinations of all the colours of the visible spectrum, so "white" noise is made up of sound energy distributed equally over the entire audio spectrum. By biasing the noise so that the sound energy is equally distributed in octaves over the entire audio spectrum, you produce what is known as "pink" noise.

Consider the octaves A-110 to A-220, and A-880 to A-1760. The former octave spans 110 integral frequencies, while the latter spans 880. In the case of white noise, over a fixed period every frequency would sound for an equal period of time; however, with pink noise every octave needs to put out an equal amount of sound energy; so, as there are eight times the number of integer frequencies in the upper octave, each will sound with one-eighth of the intensity. Having less of a high frequency component, pink noise has a less harsh quality to it than white noise. Figure 43 illustrates the frequency make-up of pink noise. The amplitude of the frequencies is attenuated by 3dB (halved) for every octave increase.

There are other varieties of noise that have been given a nomenclature – azure noise being the most common. Further discussion of this subject, however, lies in the field of acoustics rather than electronic music synthesis.

One interesting use of white noise is that of sensory deprivation. Noise can be used as an audio mask. If you amplify a white noise signal to a sufficient level, it will cover up all other sounds going on. With reference to figure 44 this becomes fairly obvious. Figure 44 a represents a sound on its own – a clock ticking for example. Add to this a random audio signal (noise) – figure 44 b – and the noise source, which contains all the frequencies in the audio spectrum virtually obliterates the ticking.

Use of high levels of white noise, in conjunction with enclosure in a pitch black room, has been used on many occasions as a form of torture.

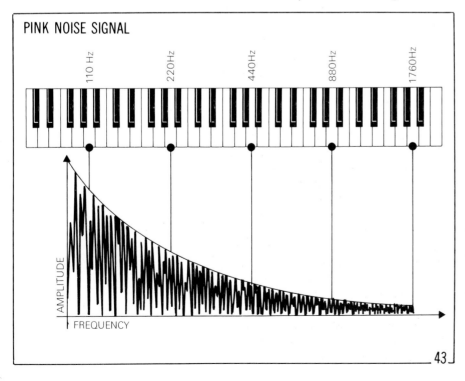

PINK NOISE SIGNAL

43

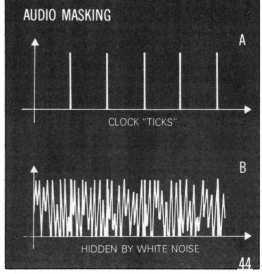

AUDIO MASKING

44

The Audio Mixer

We now have the elements from which we can construct our desired sound. But first they have to be combined to form a composite signal. So a simple audio mixer is utilised. This is simply a device that enables you to set the amplitudes of the various sound sources, and, with some instruments may not even appear as a separate set of controls, there will just be level controls and/or switches for the various sources. These drawings show a typical single oscillator/ mixer set up using rotary controls, and a dual oscillator arrangement, using slider controls.

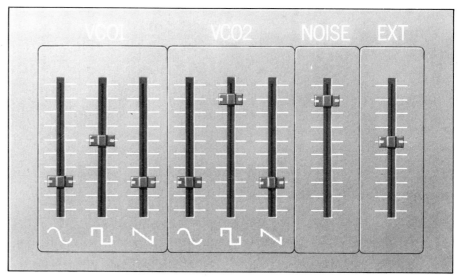

DUAL OSCILLATOR AUDIO MIXER (SLIDERS)

SINGLE OSCILLATOR AUDIO MIXER (ROTARIES)

Filters

The filter is the synthesizer voice module's tone control. It sets and shapes the tone colour of the sound, and is an extremely important element in the sound production chain of the subtractive synthesizer – for more reasons than are immediately apparent.

Timbre is the most subtle of the three elements of sound; you can quantify pitch and amplitude, but specifying the actual tone colour is by far the most difficult. There are no simple units of timbre as there are for frequency and volume.

A subtractive synthesizer operates by removing those parts of the signal that are unwanted – the filter is the removal contractor. But there's more to it than that. The filter, by its very operation, tends to colour the sound, i.e. give it a certain quality, and this quality is often a "trademark" of the particular make of subtractive synthesizer.

We can draw an analogy here between the filter and the body of, say, a violin. The body of the violin acts as a reservoir for air particles. When a string is bowed its vibrations are transmitted to the body *via* the bridge. The body of the violin resonates, and this in turn causes the adjacent air particles to be compressed and rarefied – thus the sound is transmitted.

It is not the vibrating string that is causing the air to vibrate. It is the actual way in which the body of the instrument responds to the vibrating string, and how this is transmitted to the air particles.

So we can deduce from this that a violin, such as a Stradivarius, derives its beautiful tone from the quality of construction of its body. The filter of a synthesizer acts in much the same way. Not only does it remove the unwanted frequencies, but it also adds its own characteristics to the sound. And this is one of the qualities of the whole practice of subtractive synthesis that gives the instrument its own natural feel.

The classic example of a filter's coloration of a signal is exemplified by the Minimoog. This was virtually the first performance orientated monophonic synthesizer, and it had a filter which induced an extremely warm and mellow quality into its sound.

This was a particularly desirable quality in the mid-Seventies, but has become less attractive in recent years. Oberheim use a filter in their synthesizer that gives the sound a much brassier timbre sought after by many (in particular American) rock players. The Sequential Circuits Prophet 5 was an extremely popular programmable polyphonic synthesizer at the beginning of the Eighties, primarily because of its relatively uncoloured sound, thus making it less recognisable as a "Prophet" and consequently more suited to imitative roles.

Why does one manufacturer's voice module sound different from another's? Firstly, it should be noted that it is actually the filter that is the cause. A square wave is a square wave and will sound the same no matter how it is produced,

THE PROPHET 5

so it has to be the filter stage that is responsible.

Without going into too much depth, it is all to do with the way in which the filter circuit is driven. The OSCAR synthesizer has a filter drive facility that enables you to control the amount of signal being fed into the active stages of the filter, and it is possible to hear how a more powerful signal, when fed into the filter, doesn't just come out the other end sounding louder but with its tonal colour also affected.

This can be understood to some extent by experimenting with a typical hi-fi system. Drive your system at a relatively high volume, and adjust the tone controls to get a good sound. Decrease the volume to a lower level and you notice that the bass, and to some extent the treble, frequencies become less pronounced. It doesn't sound as good. This is because your loudspeakers are not being run efficiently enough. The same basic concept is true for the filter circuitry. By driving the various elements of the circuit in different ways it is possible to alter the timbral response of the filter. Unfortunately the filter's timbral characteristics are preset by the values of the components used, and thus it is usually down to the manner in which the filter has been set-up by the designer.

Filter coloration is a very subjective subject (sic) in the same way that one type of wine might taste different from or better than another. But when one compares the sound produced by a Moog filter and an ARP filter (say), both of which are of virtually the same design (ladder filters), you should appreciate the difference in the coloration.

Enough of the esoterics, and back to exactly what a filter does, i.e. the removal of unwanted parts of a signal. There are filters in all walks of life.

Take the traffic filter. Cars wanting to turn left have a light which enables them to go, while the rest of the 'pack' who want to go straight on or right are inhibited by a stop light. This filter is allowing only left turn cars to pass.

A more elaborate kind of filter is the fisherman's trawl net, where the size of the net's mesh lets fish below a certain size escape, but retains those too big to squeeze through.

Filtering is a kind of automatic sorting process. And acoustic filters are just as straightforward in that they allow only certain frequencies to pass.

Types of Filter

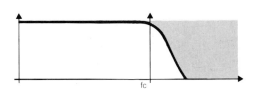

I The Low Pass Filter (LPF) – which removes frequencies above a certain value.

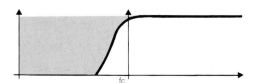

2 The High Pass Filter (HPF) – which removes frequencies below a certain value.

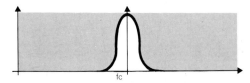

3 The Band Pass Filter (BPF) – which removes frequencies at all but a certain value.

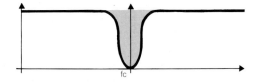

4 The Band Reject, or Notch, Filter (BRF) – which removes frequencies of a certain value.

The horizontal axis represents the frequency spectrum from low to high, and the vertical axis marks the amplitude of the filtered waveform.

We see that the lower frequencies are unaffected up to a certain frequency, f, at which point they start to be attenuated, so that very high frequencies are made virtually inaudible.

The most commonly used type of filter is the low pass because, as we've seen, the fundamental (or first harmonic) of a sound is nearly always the strongest. Thus it is necessary, more often than not, to retain the low frequency element of the sound and remove or attenuate higher harmonics. Consequently most synthesizer voice modules feature just a low pass filter.

In some instances you will find what are known as State Variable Filters. As the name implies, these are filters that can be switched to any format – low pass / high pass / band pass etc. And in some instances such a facility is useful.

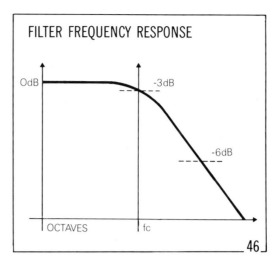

FILTER FREQUENCY RESPONSE

46

the fisherman's trawl net is not strictly accurate. It is not feasible to equip a subtractive synthesizer voice module with a filter that will alllow a frequency of, say, 100Hz to pass, but which will block a 101Hz signal.

But it is necessary to know how these higher frequencies are to be treated. That is to say we need to be able to know the "roll-off" slope, i.e. the amount by which a certain higher frequency is attenuated. Why ? Well, naturally, the amount of the higher frequency sound that is present will dictate the timbre of the overall sound.

Note that in figure 46 we have labelled the vertical amplitude axis in dBs and the horizontal frequency axis in octaves. This is convenient because the filter roll-off is measured in dBs/octave. The low pass filter used in the example exhibits a roll-off characteristic of -6dB/octave. So, say the cut-off frequency were tuned to A-440, a pitch of 880Hz would be attenuated by 6dB, and one of 1760Hz (two octaves higher) would be attenuated by 12 dB. From the first chapter you will recall that a 6dB

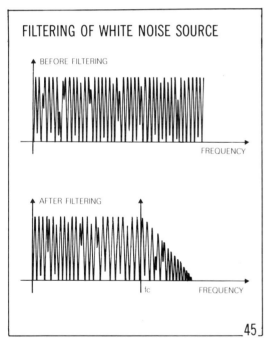

FILTERING OF WHITE NOISE SOURCE

45

Figure 45 shows a white noise source before (a), and after (b), it has been processed by a low pass filter. Those parts of the signal above frequency "fc" have, naturally enough, been attenuated. The point "fc" is known as the filter cut-off frequency and its value dramatically determines the overall effect.

Figure 46 shows what is happening at the cut-off point and above. In addition to the cut-off point "fc", another parameter affects the way in which the signal is processed – the filter's "roll-off" characteristic.

Note that those frequencies above the cut-off point don't just disappear, they are attenuated, not obliterated, so our analogy with

ROLAND SH101

attenuation results in a halving of the amplitude, and a 12dB attenuation would affect the amplitude by a factor of 4.

Figure 47 shows the effect of the same filter on a square wave of frequency 220Hz. Here you can see how the filter affects the harmonic make-up of the square wave and how the attenuation of the higher frequencies leads to a rounding off of the edges of the processed waveform.

The filters found in most music synthesizers are primarily voltage controlled, with the control voltage determining the cut-off frequency. These filters generally have a -6, -12, or -24 dBs per octave roll-off characteristic, and it is no coincidence that these are all multiples of 6, as the way in which the filter is designed dictates this. These filters are often known as 1-, 2- or 4-pole filters respectively.

There is no filter control that enables you to continually vary the roll-off characteristic of a filter. You cannot therefore tweak the filter to give a -7dB/octave response, but on some instruments provision is made to switch between, say, a 2- and 4- pole (-12/-24 dB) operation.

You may notice that there is actually a small attenuation at the cut-off frequency. This is due to the 'rounding' off caused by a transition from the OdB/octave phase (unity gain) to the -6dB response.

The most widely encountered filter is the 4-pole (24dB/octave) variety, because this gives the most dramatic attenuation of the higher frequencies. But there are occasions when you will require a less brutal attenuation, in particular for simulating brass sounds, so in these instances the 2-pole, and even the single pole, filter comes in handy.

Although we've described the above with respect to the low pass filter, the principles are applicable to the other types of filter.

Static and Dynamic Filters

A static filter is one in which the filter cut-off is set by the user and which doesn't vary with the duration of the note; similar, in fact, to the tone controls of a domestic hi-fi system. However, the cut-off frequency of a dynamic filter can be made to vary during the course of the note, thus effecting continual changes in timbre, as is the case with the sound produced by most acoustic instruments.

A typical voice module would certainly feature a low pass dynamic filter, and often a static high pass filter. The filter cut-off frequency of the dynamic filter is generally determined by a control voltage, and when we talk of VCFs (voltage controlled filters) we are usually referring to dynamic low pass filters.

Resonance and Filters

If you put an acoustic guitar in front of a microphone and turn up the volume of the amplifier, there will come a point when the loudspeaker emits a rather unpleasant howl. This is caused by a phenomenon known as feedback, and the pitch of the ensuing sonic assault is said to be the resonant frequency of the system. This feedback is caused when the sound of the guitar being picked up by the microphone is amplified to such an extent that the microphone receives a signal at a level greater than the original note. Thus the cycle repeats with the problem getting worse and worse until the system becomes unstable and we get a loud howling sound.

There is a frequency at which all systems that oscillate do so most comfortably and easily – the resonant frequency. We have already mentioned resonance with respect to acoustic theory on page 13 . Our guitar example is a similar case in question. The mass of air

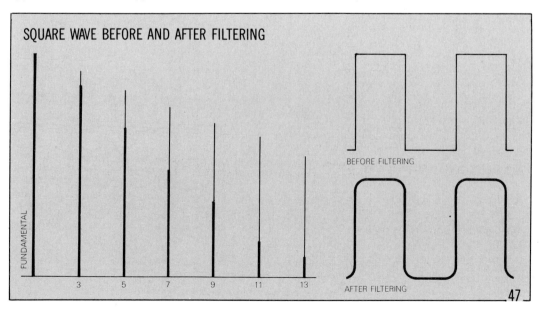

SQUARE WAVE BEFORE AND AFTER FILTERING

FUNDAMENTAL

3   5   7   9   11   13

BEFORE FILTERING

AFTER FILTERING

47

contained within the body of the guitar would like to vibrate at one particular frequency; thus when that note is played, the oscillation occurs that much more easily and the note sounds more pronounced.

The designers of the voltage controlled filters found in most subtractive synthesizers built them so as to employ feedback/resonance as a useful facility, not something as popular as leprosy. By feeding some of the output signal back into the input stage of the filter, it is possible to give the filter a resonant peak at the cut-off frequency.

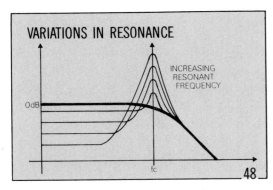

Figure 48 shows our low pass filter with varying degrees of feedback. As more and more signal is fed back to the input, so those frequencies around the cut-off frequency are actually amplified, not attenuated as one would expect a filter to do (filters ordinarily remove things, not make them bigger). Note that the amplitude of the frequencies below the cut-off point becomes more and more attenuated as the resonance/feedback increases, and in fact the actual shape of the low pass filter starts to look more and more like that of a band pass filter.

There comes a stage at which so much signal is being fed back to the input that the filter becomes 'unstable'. In fact what happens is that the filter breaks into oscillation – producing a pure sine wave of frequency "fc" that of the cut-off point. This is great because now we have a pure sine wave which we can actually use as a signal source, and of course we don't need to have a filter now since you cannot filter a pure tone, there's nothing to remove.

But how has all the this feedback affected the sound being produced? As you would expect from the above description, if the filter tends to behave more like a band pass filter when the resonance is increased, then we will hear a loss in low frequencies and a marked emphasis on those frequencies around the cut-off point.

So you can see what happens to a square wave when it is fed through a filter with increasing amounts of resonance. In this example the cut-off frequency is set at around six times the frequency of the square wave.

EFFECT OF INCREASING RESONANCE

l The basic square wave.

2 The resonance control is advanced to introduce just a small amount of feedback. You will notice that the leading edge of the waveform tends to overshoot. This small amount of resonance can be compared with what happens when you flop down on a bed. You sink into the mattress, bounce back up, then sink down a little again before coming to rest.

3 Increasing the resonance means that the square wave's leading edge overshoots quite a bit more, and the waveform fails to settle down as quickly.

4 Here the square wave is being swamped by the instability caused by the feedback – the overshoots are virtually turning the square wave into a sine wave. Note that the frequency of the superimposed waveform corresponds to the cut-off frequency of the filter.

5 The filter has now broken into oscillation, completely obliterating the square wave; all that remains is a sine wave of frequency "fc".

Resonance is an extremely important tool in creating sounds, and should be used in close conjunction with the cut-off frequency control. Together, the settings of these two parameters play the most vital part in the construction of any sound.

"Playing" the Filter

The dynamic filter is a voltage controlled device – by feeding the VCF a control voltage you can determine the cut-off frequency of a note. So if you were to take a feed from the controller voltage that is fed to the VCO, it is possible (on many synthesizers) to get the filter cut-off frequency to track the keyboard. This is important for two reasons, see figure 49.

Most synthesizers have a keyboard that spans at least 3 octaves, often up to 5. Consider the note C four octaves apart – bottom C might be around 65Hz, so the C four octaves above would be at 1040Hz (65x2x2x2x2 = 1040). Both square waves have the same harmonic structure so say we set the cut-off frequency of the filter at 520Hz.

At this stage just consider the fundamental of each waveform. The filter with "fc" at 520Hz will have no effect on the fundamental of 65Hz, but it will have quite a marked effect on the 1040Hz tone. Thus you will find that if the cut-off frequency is fixed, it will result in filtered waveform being changed across the span of the keyboard. The only way to get over this is to ensure that the cut-off frequency of the filter is directly proportional to the frequency of the note being produced.

This is done as described above by getting the filter to track the keyboard. Consequently if the cut-off frequency were set at 130Hz (twice the fundamental) for the bottom C, it would translate to 2080Hz (2x1040) by the time the top C were played.

Most sounds are not of a fixed timbre, i.e. the harmonic content varies during the course of the sound. For example, the sound of a guitar string being plucked. The sound is rich in harmonics as the note is played, but these harmonics die away fairly rapidly leaving a strong fundamental pitch during the final phase of the note.

So far we've discussed only filtering with respect to a fixed cut-off frequency, but by varying the cut-off point during the course of the note we can create a sound with harmonics of continually varying amplitude.

The VCF is a dynamic device, so if we apply a suitable voltage, we can get the cut-off point to move in tandem with the control voltage. The circuit we use to generate this control voltage is known as an envelope generator. We will deal more fully with this device as soon as we've considered the circuit that specifies the third of the three fundamental elements of sound, i.e. Loudness.

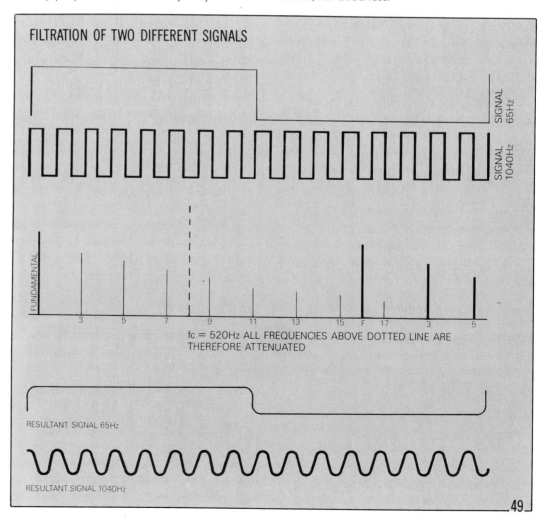

FILTRATION OF TWO DIFFERENT SIGNALS

SIGNAL 65Hz

SIGNAL 1040Hz

FUNDAMENTAL

3   5   7   9   11   13   15   F   17   3   5

fc = 520Hz ALL FREQUENCIES ABOVE DOTTED LINE ARE THEREFORE ATTENUATED

RESULTANT SIGNAL 65Hz

RESULTANT SIGNAL 1040Hz

49

The Voltage Controlled Amplifier (VCA)

This is undoubtedly the most simple of the three main voice module circuits. The VCA receives an audio signal, and amplifies it or attenuates it in proportion to a control signal applied to it. Generally this signal is a continually changing control voltage emanating from an Envelope Generator.

In figure 50 we have a sine wave being fed to a VCA and the response that the control voltage has on the output is shown in the accompanying graph. Note that the amplitude of the output is symmetrical – the VCA doesn't affect the shape of the signal in any way, just its proportions.

The Envelope Generator (EG)

This device is another building block forming part of the synthesizer voice module. All modules will have at least one envelope generator, many will have two, and occasionally you will find instruments with three per voice. The envelope generator is used to shape the sound. When it is applied to the voltage controlled filter, it shapes the timbre of the note, and when applied to the voltage controlled amplifier, it determines the amplitude of the note. On the less expensive instruments the single EG can be assigned to either the VCF or VCA, but ideally a separate EG should be incorporated for each device.

The envelope generator, sometimes known as the transient generator, produces an aperiodic waveform, i.e. a waveform that doesn't repeat itself unless actively told to do so. In this case the waveform is a single relatively simple shape and will last from between 0.1 to 25 seconds. So, as the waveform isn't continually repeating itself, it needs a signal to tell it when to start. And of course that signal is the instant a key is depressed. So, as we know, the synthesizer voice module needs two pieces of information in terms of controller data: 1) which note is played, and 2) when the respective key is played, and subsequently released.

There are many different types of envelope generator, but at this point we will deal with the two most common – others being derivatives thereof:

1) The ADSR Envelope
This type of envelope generator is most commonly found on analogue (subtractive) synthesizers, and consists of four basic phases – Attack, Decay, Sustain, Release (figure 51).

An envelope will always start at rest – i.e.

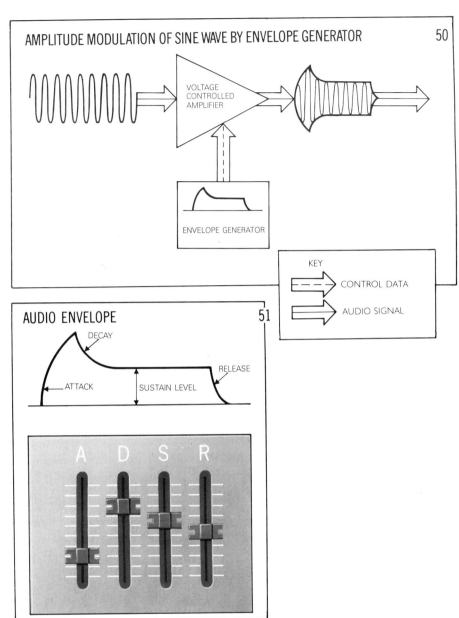

AMPLITUDE MODULATION OF SINE WAVE BY ENVELOPE GENERATOR 50

VOLTAGE CONTROLLED AMPLIFIER

ENVELOPE GENERATOR

KEY

CONTROL DATA

AUDIO SIGNAL

AUDIO ENVELOPE 51

DECAY

ATTACK

SUSTAIN LEVEL

RELEASE

A D S R

with an output of zero volts – so when connected to a voltage controlled circuit, it will have no effect until initiated ("fired").

ATTACK: Upon receipt of a signal stating that a key has been played, the envelope rises to a maximum value at a rate determined by the attack control. This is a time parameter; i.e. the more the control is advanced, the longer it takes for the voltage to reach its maximum value.

The "maximum value", as mentioned when discussing the Attack phase, is a function of the design of the envelope generator, i.e. it is a fixed value; consequently the actual size of the envelope generator is fixed. However, the effects of the envelope generator can be modified by attenuating the output voltage. This is generally done by the "Envelope Amount" control, and this in effect adjusts the value of the "maximum value".

DECAY / SUSTAIN: Upon reaching the maximum level the voltage output of the envelope generator falls back at a new rate governed by the decay control until the voltage reaches the level that corresponds to the setting of the Sustain control. The exact function of the Decay setting varies depending on the design of the instrument. Some manufacturers have the Decay control act as a time parameter so that the control sets the actual time it takes for the voltage to fall from the maximum to the Sustain level. In this case the value of the Sustain level doesn't affect the duration of the Decay phase. Others use the control to determine the rate, or 'slope', at which the envelope decays, in which case the value of the Sustain level becomes an important consideration (see figure 52).

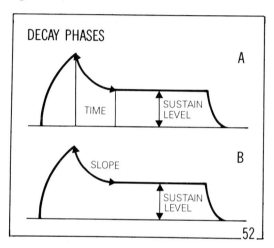

DECAY PHASES

A

TIME

SUSTAIN LEVEL

B

SLOPE

SUSTAIN LEVEL

52

EXAMPLES OF LOUDNESS ENVELOPES

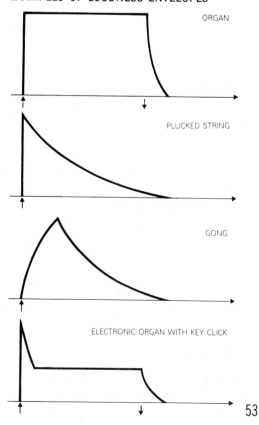

ORGAN

PLUCKED STRING

GONG

ELECTRONIC ORGAN WITH KEY CLICK

53

SUSTAIN: This is the level at which the envelope remains so long as the note is held. If it is set at zero, the envelope will fall to its original start position at a rate determined by the Decay control.

RELEASE: Upon release of the note, the envelope falls away to its original starting value at a rate determined by the Release control. As with the Decay phase, this can be either a fixed time parameter, so that the time period between the release of the key and the return of the envelope to its initial start point is set by the control, or rate parameter, when the 'slope' of the release phase is designated.

Figure 53 shows a range of different envelopes possible with ADSR.

There are variations on the ADSR theme. Some less expensive instruments feature AD, AR, or ADS envelopes which by their very nature are less flexible than the ADSR variety.

The AD (Attack-Decay) envelope, upon receipt of a trigger pulse, rises at a rate determined by the Attack control, and then, upon reaching the maximum value, falls back at the Decay rate. Sustaining the note has no effect. This is a percussive envelope.

The AR (Attack-Release) envelope rises to the maximum value, then sits there while the note is held until the key is released, then falls away at a rate set by the Release control. This is a sustained envelope.

The ADSD (Attack-Decay-Sustain-Decay) envelope functions in much the same way as the ADSR envelope; only the Release phase has exactly the same characteristics as the Decay phase, and the same control setting is used for both parameters.

There are other hybrid envelope generators offering more than the basic ADSR phases. The DADSR envelope features a Delay ("D"ADSR) control that introduces a time delay in between the triggering of the note and the initiation of the Attack phase. This can be extremely useful when the filter is being used to modulate the envelope generator as a slight delay can add considerable depth to the overall perception of the sound.

Other 'deviations' on the ADSR theme include Repeat facilities, which enable the envelope to retrigger itself, thus no longer generating a true aperiodic waveform, but a regularly repeating waveshape.

2) The RL (Rate-Level) Envelope.
The Rate-Level envelope generator is in essence a much simpler device. But it can be used to produce a far wider range of envelopes.

The system functions by specifying a number of points in the envelope, the Levels, and deciding how long you want the voltage to take in moving between these points, the Rates.

Figure 54 shows a simple four stage RL envelope. The activation of a note causes the output to rise from a base to Level 1 (LI) and it takes the set time Rate 1 (RI) to get there. The voltage then proceeds to Level 2 (L2) in a time set by the value of Rate 2 (R2). The pattern continues in a similar fashion until the envelope reaches Level 3. At this point the output of the envelope generator remains steady until the note is released, and then the envelope moves to Level 4 at Rate 4. Level 4 is the resting value for the envelope. It is from this level that the envelope is activated when a note is played, and the 'Attack' phase equates to Rate 1 – the time it takes to move from L4 to LI. For most purposes L4 is usually set at zero.

The RL envelope system is an immensely flexible one, primarily because you are specifying 8 parameters (rather than 4 as with the ADSR EG), but also because it allows you to set up a considerably wider range of shapes. Figure 55 shows such a range.

There are several variations on the theme of the RL envelope. Some envelopes, employing 6 or 8 stages, actually enable you to specify on which level you want the envelope to sustain. Consequently it is possible to create an amazingly dexterous waveshape – albeit somewhat unnatural in shape.

Although it would seem far more flexible than the ADSR envelope, the RL often sounds less natural and more clinical than the ADSR variety, and using the RL is considerably more long-winded than the straightforward ADSR circuit.

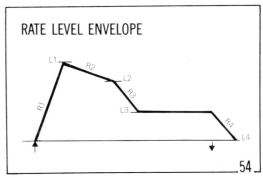

RATE LEVEL ENVELOPE

54

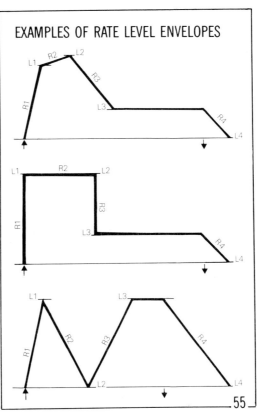

EXAMPLES OF RATE LEVEL ENVELOPES

55

Low Frequency Oscillator (LFO)

There is one main facet of the Subtractive Synthesizer's voice module that hasn't yet been discussed, and that's the low frequency oscillator.

The LFO, although it oscillates, doesn't normally actually make any sound. It operates in a frequency band that is below that of the audible frequency spectrum – generally between around 0.1 Hz (one cycle every 10 seconds) up to roughly 35 Hz (which is just breaking the threshold of the audible spectrum, but only just).

The LFO is used to generate voltages that modify other voltage controlled elements – most notably the oscillators and the filters. So if you wanted to continually vary any particular parameter, you would use the LFO.

This is not usually a voltage controllable device, so the LFO's frequency is a static one. A simple frequency control sets this rate.

A good LFO will generate at least four separate output waveforms: Sine, Ramp Up, Ramp Down, and Square. A Triangle wave is sometimes used as a substitute for the sine wave as it is electronically simpler to generate.

As we shall see, the LFO is a vital part of the electronic music synthesizer voice module; however, some polyphonic instruments share a single LFO with all the voice modules. This is understandable as it keeps down costs, and those occasions when you need a separate LFO for each module don't often occur. Those instruments that do use more than one VCO (or DCO) per voice often provide the facility with which one or more of the extra oscillators can be switched to become low frequency oscillators, and thus used as control elements rather than for sound producing.

Sample-and-Hold

Some LFO's offer a Sample-and-Hold output, a strange facility, but an extremely useful one. The Sample-and-Hold waveform is a completely random waveform, but "quantised" into time packages, the duration of which is determined by the LFO.

Figure 56 explains things a little more clearly. The LFO runs at a certain frequency, say 1 cycle per second (1Hz). A constantly changing signal is fed to the LFO, and this can be either a pitched sound (a) or a totally random one (b). At the beginning of each cycle, the LFO looks at this signal and freezes the signal's level at that voltage level for the duration of the cycle. It then looks at the new current position of the signal, and adopts that value for the duration of the cycle. The result is a relatively random waveform (depending on the nature of the source signal), but one that is divided into equal time steps. The Sample-and-Hold waveform, by its very nature, has a random feel to it but because the waveform is fragmented into steps the waveform has a rhythmic quality to it, especially if used at a suitable frequency (say 2-6Hz).

The Voice Module Revisited

We are now in a position to assemble all the building blocks that make up the voice module, and consider the complete entity – figure 57 (as depicted in figure 32 p. 38).

We can see more clearly how the signal flows; the various elements dividing themselves

up into Carriers, devices that do the work in creating or directly determining one of three prime elements (the VCOs, VCF and VCA) and Modifiers, devices which change the carriers (the EGs and LFOs). Now we can consider more carefully the way in which the various blocks interact with one another.

We have three basic elements: pitch, timbre and loudness. These are taken care of by the VCO(s)/DCO(s), VCF, and VCA respectively.

We have two ways in which each of these elements can be automatically changed: periodically, or aperiodically (utilising the cycling LFO waveform, or the "one-off" envelope).

We therefore need to consider the various permutations:

1 periodic variation of pitch (LFO+VCO)
2 periodic variation of timbre (LFO+VCF)
3 periodic variation of loudness (LFO+VCA)
4 aperiodic variation of pitch (EG+VCO)
5 aperiodic variation of timbre (EG+VCF)
6 aperiodic variation of loudness (EG+VCA)

The most important of which is undoubtedly the last – EG+VCA.

EG (modifier) and VCA (carrier).

Question – what happens if the amplitude of a sound remains constant? Answer – the sound just drones on and on indefinitely. All sounds have continually changing amplitudes. A church organ emits no sound until a note is played (loudness=0). The amplitude then shoots up to a maximum value for that note (loudness=x) where it remains until the note is released, whence the amplitude rapidly falls back to zero (loudness=0). It's clear that

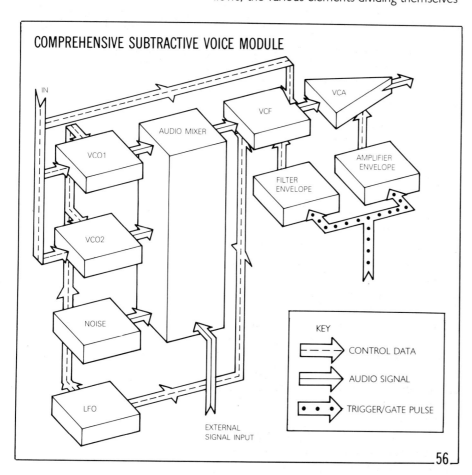

SAMPLE AND HOLD WAVEFORM

SIGNAL

LOW FREQUENCY OSCILLATOR

RESULTANT

57

COMPREHENSIVE SUBTRACTIVE VOICE MODULE

IN

VCA

VCF

AUDIO MIXER

VCO1

AMPLIFIER ENVELOPE

FILTER ENVELOPE

VCO2

NOISE

LFO

EXTERNAL SIGNAL INPUT

KEY

CONTROL DATA

AUDIO SIGNAL

TRIGGER/GATE PULSE

56

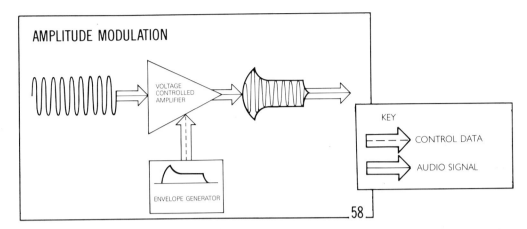

AMPLITUDE MODULATION

VOLTAGE CONTROLLED AMPLIFIER

ENVELOPE GENERATOR

KEY

- - - → CONTROL DATA

⇒ AUDIO SIGNAL

58

the amplitude of the note is changing, shaped by an envelope waveform. A VCA on a synthesizer is virtually useless unless controlled by an envelope generator.

Figure 58 shows how an ADSR envelope modifies the signal applied to the VCA. It simply shapes it to produce the desired effect. It is important that the envelope voltage returns to a zero level otherwise the voltage controlled amplifier will not "close down" and you will find that a small amount of the audio signal being fed to the VCA will bleed through. This was a constant problem with some of the earlier polyphonic instruments, and if you were to listen closely, when no notes were being played, an effect known as bee-hiving would occur. This was caused by tiny residue output tones from all the voice modules, all at different pitches, combining to produce a composite signal rather like that which emanates from a hive of bees.

Voltage Controlled Amplifiers respond to the voltage applied to them in two distinct ways – Linearly and Exponentially.

Linear response causes a straight line graph, which means that the amplitude increases in direct proportion to the voltage. Nature doesn't believe in straight lines, however, so in order to achieve a smooth variation of amplitude and voltage an exponential relationship is actually more suitable. The differences between the two types of response are seldom critical in basic electronic musical synthesis.

EG (modifier) and VCF (carrier)

The use of the envelope generator with the filter is another vitally important element in the working of the synthesizer voice module. As mentioned earlier, all acoustic sounds have a constantly changing harmonic content. We could play a note on the synthesizer and twiddle the filter cut-off frequency knob to produce the desired tonal response, but in almost all cases this is most unsatisfactory. Instead, why not get the envelope generator to do all the work. The envelope generator is triggered every time a note is played, and the cut-off frequency

ROLAND MODULAR SYNTHESIZER MPG-80

follows the voltage produced. And so those unwanted harmonics are removed.

Ideally a voice module should be equipped with two envelope generators, one for the VCF the other for the VCA, but sometimes the price of the instrument dictates a single EG be shared between both circuits. In this case, either both voltage controlled elements receive the same envelope, or a gate pulse is used as a second EG for controlling one of the elements – usually the VCA. The gate pulse is a simple ON/OFF envelope which rises from rest when a key is pressed to a maximum level, where it stays until the note is released, whence it falls back to the original position. In this case one could envisage the use of ADSR and Gate envelopes as shown in figure 59.

When using the EG to vary the pitch with time, there are two important considerations: how much envelope do I use and about what

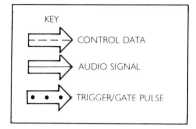

KEY
CONTROL DATA
AUDIO SIGNAL
TRIGGER/GATE PULSE

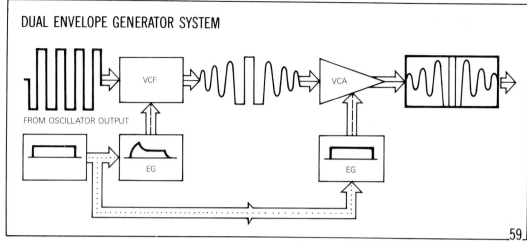

DUAL ENVELOPE GENERATOR SYSTEM

FROM OSCILLATOR OUTPUT

VCF   VCA   EG   EG

59

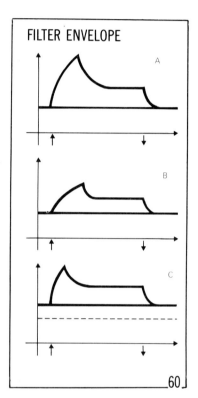

FILTER ENVELOPE

A

B

C

60

frequency do I bias it ? Figure 60 should clear up any confusion caused by this question. In Figure 60 (a) we see the voltage produced by the envelope generator. Now this causes the cut-off frequency to move from its initial position to a new one. The initial position is still set by the filter's cut-off frequency control, and the maximum amount this moves under control from the EG is determined by the envelope amount control. So different combinations of these are illustrated in figures 60 (b) and 60 (c).

The resonance control is not a voltage controlled parameter; therefore it remains at its set value during the course of the note.

The typical "booiiwwing" type of sound is that of a filter (with a high resonance) being swept by an envelope generator, but much more subtle use can be made of the sets of controls.

Many synthesizers offer the facility of inverting the envelope so that as the note is played the cut-off point can be made to move down the frequency spectrum, rather than up.

EG (modifier) and VCO (carrier)
A voltage when applied to a voltage controlled filter changes the pitch of the output – true. But with some instruments there is another voltage controlled parameter associated with the oscillator – that's the pulse width. A voltage can be used to alter the duty cycle of the pulse width.

So by applying an envelope generator to the pulse width element you can change the harmonic structure of the oscillator's output, and thus you are in effect changing the sound's timbre. See figure 61. The effect is somewhat different from that of sweeping the VCF with the EG, but the effect can be compared. If you start with a pulse width with around a 50% duty cycle (almost a square wave), the sound is relatively strong in low frequency harmonics, but as the envelope rises, the pulse becomes increasingly narrow and sounds thinner because

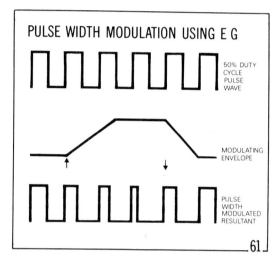

PULSE WIDTH MODULATION USING E G

50% DUTY CYCLE PULSE WAVE

MODULATING ENVELOPE

PULSE WIDTH MODULATED RESULTANT

61

the low frequency elements have been removed.

When considering the modulation of the oscillator's pitch by the envelope generator, again, it is the oscillator's frequency control that dictates the point about which the envelope is going to operate, and the EG Amount control determines how much pitch movement the envelope generator is going to induce.

The use of the envelope generator to sweep the frequency is not that often used, except for special effects etc. Although a tiny hint of EG induced pitch sweep is useful when creating simulations of the human voice, or choir effects. In these instances the pitch of the VCO(s) would be set a little below the correct tuning, and as the note was played the envelope generator's pitch would bring the note up into tune, where it would stay until released.

LFO (modifier) and VCA (carrier)
There's a rather more friendly name for one variety of periodic variation of amplitude with time – tremolo. Tremolo is amplitude modulation using a low frequency sine wave. Figure 62 shows what's going on. The audio signal is simply amplified and attenuated by amounts directly in proportion to the sine wave, and the effect is a pulsating, yet smooth

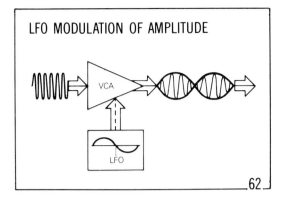

LFO MODULATION OF AMPLITUDE

62

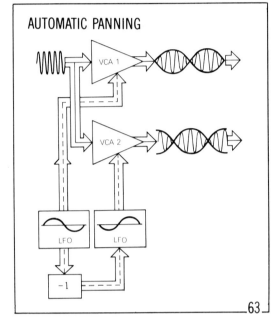

AUTOMATIC PANNING

63

change in volume. If a square wave is used as the LFO waveform then the effect is one of jumping between two volume levels.

Take a situation as shown in figure 63. Here we have the same audio signal being fed to two VCAs. One VCA is being fed by a straight sine wave and the other by an inverted sine wave (an inverted sine wave is half a cycle out of phase with a non inverted one, so when one is high, the other is low). The effect of this configuration is to bounce the signal back and forth between the two VCAs output, so that when one output is loud the other is quiet. This set-up is known as automatic panning, and was used to great effect in the old Fender Rhodes Suitcase pianos (though in fact the effect was wrongly labelled a stereo vibrato circuit – it should have been a stereo tremolo).

LFO (modifier) and VCF (carrier)

"Wow" and "Growl" are terms that used to be associated with the periodic modulation of the voltage controlled filter. The low frequency oscillator is seldom used to modulate the filter because it seldom (if ever) appears in the acoustic world. It was, however, for this very reason that the effect was used quite heavily in the Sixties and early Seventies. Why? Because

this kind of sound had never been heard before – but like the fuzz box, and flange pedal, the effect became overplayed, and gradually phased itself out.

LFO (modifier) and VCO (carrier)

This is one of the most important aspects of varying the sound as the note is played. As with aperiodic variation of pitch with time, there are two different ways in which the low frequency modulation can be used:

1 to vary the pitch of the oscillator
2 to vary the oscillator's pulse width.

Such is the importance of 1) that a performance control is actually used to introduce LFO modulation during the course of the note.

Figure 64 shows the square wave output from an oscillator. The modulation from the LFO causes the waveform to rise and fall in pitch, and this compresses and expands the waveform, though its actual shape doesn't change.

If a sine wave is used as the modulating waveform we have a resultant wave-train as shown in figure 64 a. This is known as vibrato, and is extensively used. On the other hand, Trill employs the square wave output of the LFO as the modulating source. Think what is happening in this situation. We are applying a signal (the square wave) that exists in two states – high and low. What will it do to the pitch of the carrier oscillator? This will, of course, oscillate between two pitches as shown diagrammatically in figure 64 b. Trill is not very often used because it is, of course, relatively easy to play a trill on the keyboard.

Other waveforms are used as modulating sources, but primarily only for special effects, e.g. warning sirens etc.

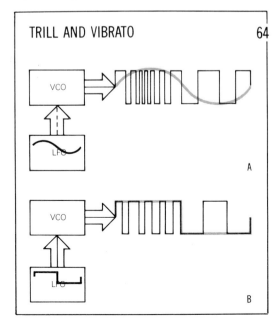

TRILL AND VIBRATO
64

A

B

The use of one frequency to modulate another is known as frequency modulation and does, in fact, form a basis for a whole genre of synthesizers – FM Digital Synthesis – see p. 61.

The low frequency oscillator can also adopt an extremely useful role when varying the pulse width of a waveform. The effect, if set up correctly, is akin to the beating of two oscillators, and this pulse width modulation, as it is called, is a device used by manufacturers to "beef" up the sound of 'one oscillator per voice' synthesizers. In this instance it is only the LFO's sine (or triangle) wave outputs that are used. By constantly varying the width of a pulse waveform around once a second, you can create that rich phase-cancelling effect with one oscillator.

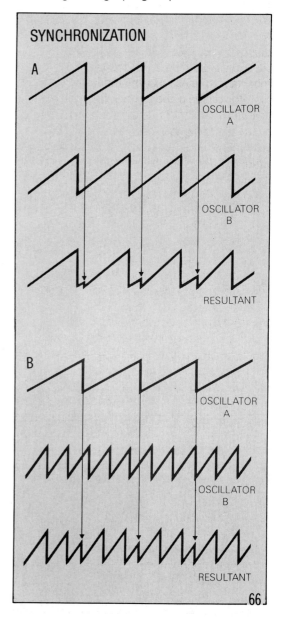

Hybrid Facilities

The voice modules of some more elaborate synthesizers may be equipped with certain extra "building blocks" to facilitate more precise control over the sound. The following are the most commonly encountered:

Digital Waveform Oscillators
There are digitally controlled oscillators, and digital oscillators. The former, (DCOs), have their frequency determined by a digital control code rather than by a control voltage; while the DWOs, though they too are digitally controlled, actually create their waveforms digitally. Consider figure 65. Here we see a sine wave, but look closely and you see that it isn't a smoothly varying waveform, but a series of horizontal/vertical zig-zags. You may have noticed that this is how computers draw circles and curves on their screens.

What exactly is happening is that the sine wave is being split up into a large number of vertical time-slices each of the same width. Each slice has a specific height, and by specifying this height for each of these slices as a number, and listing them sequentially, it is possible to represent the sine wave digitally. By this method any waveform can be represented as a string of numbers.

The greater the number of slices the closer the digital approximation becomes to an analogue waveform. Usually there are at least 256 slices to a complete cycle of a waveform. Frequency is determined by the width of each slice – if the slice is thin, the complete waveform doesn't last for very long, and the pitch is high.

Don't be put off by the fact that the actual waveform is jagged rather than smooth. If you have as many as 256 steps in the cycle, these edges will have virtually no effect on the

perceived sound, in the same way as the lines on a television screen seem to disappear when the whole picture is viewed from a few feet away.

The strings of numbers that constitute the various digital waveforms are preprogrammed into the synthesizer's memory, so complex waveforms can be used as the source, as a direct replacement of the simpler triangle, ramp or square waves. These then are subsequently processed by the other circuit elements . . . VCF, VCA etc.

Synchronization
This facility is applicable only to voice modules with two or more VCOs/DCOs. Synchronization refers to the locking of one oscillator on to a harmonic of the other's output.

Figure 66a shows two sawtooth waveforms, one oscillating (OSC-A) at a frequency of 200Hz say, whilst a second oscillator (OSC-B) is running at a slightly higher pitch. If, now,

OSC-B were to be synchronized to OSC-A, the waveform shown would ensue.

Synchronization means that OSC-B is 'reset' every time OSC-A resets. Thus we get a new waveform with frequency the same as that of OSC-A, but of a completely different shape, and with 'slopes' the same as OSC-B. The actual sound of two synchronized sounds is in fact dull and flat – obviously so, as there's no movement between the waveforms. You are creating one waveform from two others. However, by changing the frequency of OSC-B one can create some amazing harmonic effects. This can be shown visually by considering figure 66b. Look how complex the resultant synchronization waveform has become as a result of raising the frequency of OSC-B.

Cross Modulation

Cross Modulation, like synchronization, is applicable only to voice modules with two or more VCOs/DCOs. Basically it involves the frequency modulation of one oscillator by another. The modulating oscillator is usually switchable so that it can operate either: i) in the audible frequencies, or ii) as a low frequency oscillator. In both instances though, it is important to realise that the modulating oscillator can be made to track the controller, i.e. both oscillators will move in pitch depending on the note being played.

CASE 1). Using two 'high' frequency oscillators is a very crude simulation of FM Synthesis. The modulation results in a composite waveform that is very rich in harmonics, and is particularly useful for bell like effects, and metallic sounds.

CASE 2). Using one of the VCOs as an LFO might on the surface seem a little extravagant – all synthesizers have an LFO, so why lose a VCO at the expense of duplication ? The answer becomes valid only if you are considering a polyphonic synthesizer, where generally there is just one LFO which is shared

THE CONTROL PANEL

by all the voice modules. Here, say you were using the LFO for pitch modulation, all voices would rise at the same time and fall at the same time, which, if you were trying to simulate a string section, obviously wouldn't sound authentic. But if you have a separate LFO for each voice, then the modulation for each note will not be phase related to any of the other notes, thus the effect will be far more authentic. See figure 67.

Cross Filter Modulation

A particularly interesting form of modulation occurs when the VCF's cut-off frequency is modulated by a VCO/DCO running at a high frequency. Not many synthesizers offer this facility (Sequential Inc. seem to promote this facility most). By increasing the resonance almost to the point of oscillation, and biasing the cut-off point to a relatively low frequency, and by applying aperiodic modulation from the envelope generator, it is possible to get a talking bullfrog type of sound which gets well away from the traditional range of subtractive synthesis sounds.

Ring Modulation

A third category of modulation that applies only to those instruments that have two or more oscillators is Ring Modulation. This was a popular facility in the early days of the synthesizer when you would find RM circuits on modular instruments and some of the more effect orientated performance instruments, but the popularity of this facility waned. More recently, with the increasing vogue for metallic sounds, RM has started to reappear.

This is an arithmetic circuit which takes two frequencies from the two oscillators and produces two other pitches – one being the sum of the two frequencies, the other being the difference. So if we fed a tone at A-440 and another A two octaves down, at 110Hz into the ring modulator, we would get out a tone of 550Hz (the sum) and one of 330Hz (the difference).

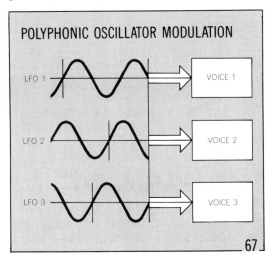

POLYPHONIC OSCILLATOR MODULATION

LFO 1 → VOICE 1

LFO 2 → VOICE 2

LFO 3 → VOICE 3

67

Static High Pass Filter

In order to effect a more exacting harmonic content, many manufacturers incorporate a static high pass filter in the signal chain (as shown in figure 68). This gives the user a way in which he can control both the high frequency (VCF low pass) and low frequency (static high pass) make-up of the sound. This filter has just one control parameter which sets the cut-off frequency, blocking those frequencies above that point.

If you take away the low frequency element of a sound you are left with a relatively thin sound, so this control is primarily used for voices such as oboes and recorders etc.

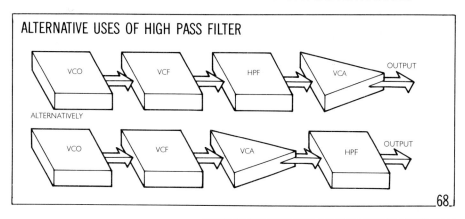

ALTERNATIVE USES OF HIGH PASS FILTER

68

We've now seen how the various blocks in the subtractive voice module work together to construct the sound. We will be dealing later with use of the controller, performance controls and use of the synthesizer. These subjects are relevant to most of the types of synthesizers under discussion. Therefore it is perhaps astute to look at the other forms of synthesis before discussing the instrument's implementation.

Hybrid Voltage Controlled Filters

We've already seen that the VCF is critical in determining the timbral quality of an instrument's sound. So far the two most important designs have been the 'ladder' (the term refers to its circuit construction) type of low pass filter – used by Moog and ARP in the early days – and the state variable filter, which can be used to create low, high, band, or notch filter configurations. The actual quality of the sound emanating from these kinds of filters has depended on how the circuits have been driven and biased.

Recently one or two companies have opted to use the dual-peak filter. This is equivalent to having two filters linked in tandem so that there are, in effect, two cut-off points. This may seem a contradiction in terms, but what it does is to enable a frequency plot as shown in figure 69

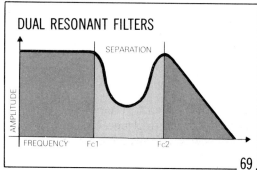

DUAL RESONANT FILTERS

69

to be created. You will notice that there is, as the circuit's name implies, a second peak to the response.

The effect of this peak is to enrich the sound considerably and to make the filter more flexible. An extra control is included which sets the separation between the two cut-off points – both of which move in tandem depending on the modulating control voltage applied to the filter.

It is known that our vocal cavity has two characteristic resonant frequencies, so it is obvious that synthesizers offering dual peak filters are extremely good at creating voice-like sounds.

ADDITIVE & FM SYNTHESIS

5

Additive Synthesis

An additive synthesizer, as the name implies, starts from scratch and builds up a sound by adding together waveforms. Gone are the 'traditional' building blocks of VCOs, VCFs and VCAs, instead we have theoretical (explained later) banks of sine wave generators that are used as the pieces in the construction of our sound.

We have already seen in essence how the additive synthesizer voice module works. Harmonics, in the form of sine waves of different pitch and amplitude, can be summed to form new waveforms and it can be shown that virtually any waveform can be constructed in this manner. The impracticality is that a very large number of sine wave generators are required.

This principle, which forms the backbone of the subject of additive synthesis, is attributed to Joseph Fourier – a 19th century physicist. His studies had nothing whatsoever to do with music, but he did establish his "Theory of Superposition", which in simple terms stipulated that any waveform could be broken down into a number of sine waves, each of a fixed pitch and amplitude.

The first real commercial musical application of Fourier's work was Hammond drawbar organs. Here we had nine harmonics that could be mixed together in different amounts to produce a myriad of different tones. (See p.14).

We can create any waveform using banks of sine wave generators, but this, as we've seen when dealing with subtractive synthesis, isn't the end of the story. An electronic music synthesizer has to be able to produce sounds whose amplitude, timbre, and in certain instances pitch, vary over the course of the note. Consequently the waveforms produced by the additive synthesizer have to be constantly changing in their harmonic content – a more challenging proposition.

Consider a simple sound: a tone of frequency F that starts as a square wave,

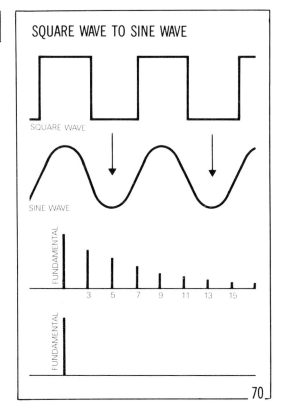

SQUARE WAVE TO SINE WAVE

SQUARE WAVE

SINE WAVE

FUNDAMENTAL

3   5   7   9   11   13   15

FUNDAMENTAL

70

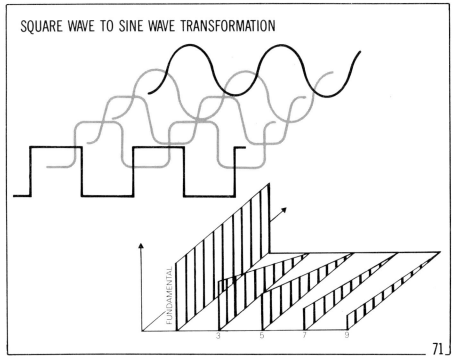

SQUARE WAVE TO SINE WAVE TRANSFORMATION

FUNDAMENTAL

3   5   7   9

71

then gradually turns into a sine wave as the note progresses. The start and finish waveforms are shown in figure 70a, and the corresponding harmonic spectra in figure 70b. A square wave is created from the formula $F + 3F/3 + 5F/5 + 7F/7$ etc. So to create a good square wave we need at least eight sine wave generators, each set to produce an odd harmonic in decreasing amplitudes. The eighth generator will therefore be producing a pitch at 15 times the fundamental frequency and 1/15th the amplitude.

Now in order that the tone can be turned into a simple sine wave over its duration, the amplitude of all the harmonics, with the exception of the fundamental, have to be reduced to zero. This gives rise to a three-dimensional plot as shown in figure 71. In effect, therefore, we need to be able to determine the amplitude and the pitch of every sine wave at every instant in time in order to create the desired sound.

"Look-up" tables

Modern additive synthesizers are not, in fact, crammed full of sine wave circuits, although from the final result it appears as if they were. Instead you will find that digital circuitry is used throughout. Sine waves are stored as digital numbers in the instrument's memories in what are known as "look-up" tables. For every instant in time, the instrument's processor is looking up where in its cycle each particular sine wave should be, and then summing together the relevant numbers to produce a train of

digits. The final stage is the digital to analogue convertor (DAC), which turns these numbers into an analogue signal. And that's all there is to it. The general term that covers this digital manipulation and final output via a DAC of an audio line signal is known as *direct synthesis*.

Generally speaking an average additive synthesizer will be using the "look-up" tables around 30,000 times a second, so if our fundamental frequency were 110Hz, then it would be made up of around 250 sets of numbers. Today's technology is primarily based on 8-bit microprocessors (processors that manipulate 8 binary digit numbers) so each step could have a binary number from '00000000' (0) to '11111111' (256), a resolution of 1:256. If we were to use only 4-bit numbers, which admittedly would use far less memory (an important commercial consideration), then the resolution of the sine wave would be 1:32, figure 72a. This would result in a sine wave that looked like the one shown in figure 72b, the distortion of which could easily be detected by the human ear.

Figure 73 shows how the above example of the square to sine wave sound is treated. For simplicity's sake, let's just consider the first, third and fifth harmonics (remember, no even harmonics are used in the construction of a square wave).

●The Fundamental (F). This remains constant throughout the course of the sound, so we get a simple train of numbers that repeat themselves over a period of time.

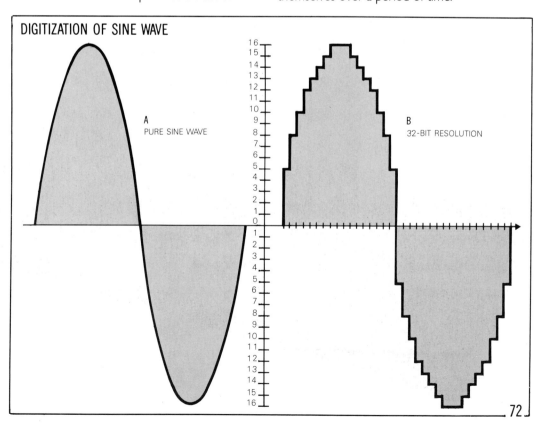

DIGITIZATION OF SINE WAVE

A
PURE SINE WAVE

B
32-BIT RESOLUTION

72

● Third Harmonic (3F/3). The look-up tables will present a set of numbers that reflect the fact that the waveform is oscillating at three times the frequency. The central processor will also have been told that this harmonic has initially to be attenuated by a factor of 3. Thus the initial numbers will be adjusted accordingly, and this factor will rise as the harmonic dies away, until a chain of zeros represents the complete attenuation of the waveform.

● Fifth Harmonic (5F/5). This follows a similar pattern to 2) above, save that a waveform five times the fundamental frequency has to be looked up and that the attenuation starts from a factor of 5.

The three-dimensional plot of the figure depicted in figure 73 shows the relative amplitude of each of the harmonics. If we were to slice through this plot with the line AA, and look face on at the section, we would see our familiar harmonic spectrum diagram at that instant in time. Note that we would get a completely different picture a fraction of a second later if we took a slice BB.

Additive digital synthesis is a useful technique that explores many new areas that cannot be reached with subtractive synthesis, but it is only when we come to hybrid versions of this subject that the power of using numbers as the tools to create sound becomes really apparent.

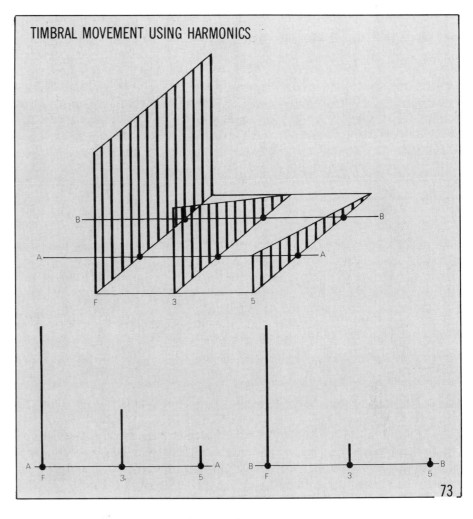

TIMBRAL MOVEMENT USING HARMONICS

73

Frequency Modulation (FM) Synthesis

The topic of frequency modulation (FM) has already cropped up when dealing with the voltage controlled oscillators of subtractive synthesis (p. 35); but in the context of the digital hybrid synthesizer, frequency modulation graduates from a simple technique to a comprehensive form of electronic music synthesis.

Frequency modulation is simply the use of one waveform to change the pitch of another. There's nothing new about FM, in fact we've experienced it in our every day lives for the past 40 or so years (assuming that's biologically possible) in the form of radio broadcasts.

An FM radio transmission utilises a "Carrier" waveform that operates around the 100 MHz region, that is 100 million cycles per second.

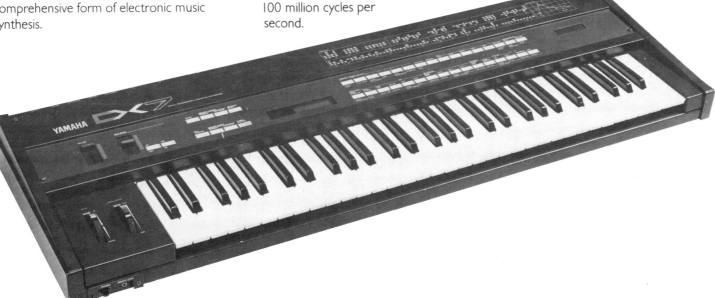

The radio program, which usually contains signals that fall within the audio spectrum (say 40-14000Hz), is known as the Modulator, and when 'loaded' on to the Carrier, causes its frequency to vary between say 99.95Hz and 100.05Hz (the exact figures depend on the depth of modulation). This modulated waveform is then sent off to the antennae and transmitted. Why is this done? Because a very high frequency can be transmitted through the ether over considerable distances.

A radio receiver picks up the signal and removes the Carrier to leave just the Modulator – which hopefully corresponds to the original programme.

FM Synthesis is a variation on this principle, but in this instance both the frequencies in question are in the audio spectrum. If you frequency modulate one audio tone with another of different pitch and amplitude, you get a completely new sound that has little audible similarity to its forebears. The trick is to know what, when modulated with what, gives what.

The man who deserves the largest share of the acclaim for pioneering FM Synthesis was Dr. John M. Chowning, then Director at the Centre for Computer Research and Music Acoustics, which formed part of Stanford University, California. Chowning, with the assistance of Dr. Max Mathews, Director of the Acoustic and Behavioral Research Centre at Bell Telephone Laboratories in New Jersey, postulated in a 1973 Audio Engineering Society paper entitled "The Synthesis of Complex Audio Spectra by Means of Frequency Modulation" that a new method of generating musical timbres was possible, and that it opened new doors to the electronic musician.

The original development system employed

by Chowning and Mathews was slow and cumbersome to use, requiring an extremely large mainframe computer to handle all the functions.

Having been convinced of the commercial feasibility of the system, Yamaha took out a licence on Chowning's patents, and after 5 years of research into digital technology, Yamaha unveiled in 1980, the first of their instruments to utilise this new technique – the GS-1.

From this expensive preset instrument evolved one of the very few 'classic' electronic instruments, one which was, and remains, a landmark in music synthesis history – the DX-7.

FM – The Basics

FM Synthesis is not an easy subject to grasp. For that reason FM Synthesizer manufacturers have always ensured that their instruments can be used with "factory preset" sounds so that those with a less adventurous nature can still get a considerable amount out of one of these instruments.

For the power which FM Synthesis offers, the hardware demands it makes are surprisingly simple. Like additive synthesis FM is all about sine waves and envelope generators, but instead

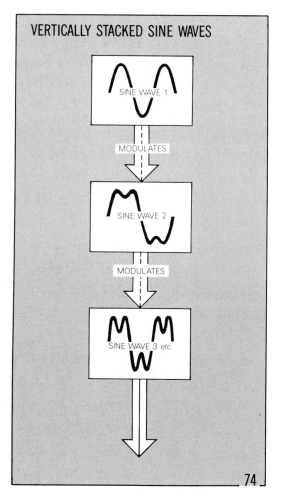

74

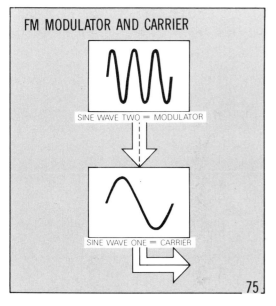

SINE WAVE TWO = MODULATOR

SINE WAVE ONE = CARRIER

75

of working horizontally, and mixing together sine waves of different amplitudes and frequencies, FM relies primarily on what happens when the sine waves are arranged vertically. Figure 74.

FM is one form of Non-linear Synthesis – yes, more subdivisions. In figure 75 we have one of the most basic FM configurations, with two sine waves oscillating in the audio spectrum. S-1 is the Carrier, and S-2 the Modulator. Now if we listen just to S-1, there are two parameters that will dramatically affect the oscillator's output, and hence its timbre:

1 the ratio between the pitch of S-1 and S-2
2 the amount of S-2 used to modulate S-1.

So far we've dealt only with a static situation, but, as we've seen, a synthesizer has to be able to produce notes with:

● amplitudes that vary with time
● timbres that vary with time
● pitches that vary with time (less important)

Solutions

The answer is to bring in an envelope generator or two. To vary the amplitude with time we simply need to regulate the volume of the Carrier (S-1) with an envelope generator – thus acting like a simple volume circuit. To control the timbre we can opt to vary either 1) or 2) above, but by simply controlling the output level of the Modulator using an envelope generator, we can achieve the desired effect and the changes in timbre will follow the contour of the envelope. As the envelope rises so does the output of the Modulator, consequently the Carrier is more heavily modulated. To vary the pitch of a note simply requires the direct modulation of the Carrier by an envelope generator.

The Operator

The above solutions give rise to the obvious 'construction' of a theoretical circuit known as an operator. Figure 76 illustrates an Operator, which consists of a variable frequency sine wave generator, a variable amplifier and an envelope generator. There are three sets of input data to which the Operator must respond: Pitch/Frequency data; Modulation data; and Envelope parameter data. From these three sets of information the operator will produce what in essence will be a sine wave of amplitude proportional to the envelope data, and of frequency corresponding to the pitch data. But by virtue of the modulation data, the shape of the sine wave may be 'distorted' and made completely unrecognisable.

Figure 77 shows a simple Operator configuration, where Operator 2 is feeding its continually varying sine wave output into the modulation port of the Carrier, Operator 1. This "wiring diagram" of operators is known as an Algorithm. In this case we have stacked one operator on top of another, i.e. we are modulating 1 with 2. This is known as "series linking" of Operators. If we were simply to use both Operators side by side as Carriers (figure 78), i.e. mix together the two sine wave outputs, we would have what is known as "parallel linking". This latter format is identical

KEY

PARAMETER DATA

CONTROL DATA

AUDIO SIGNAL

TRIGGER/GATE PULSE

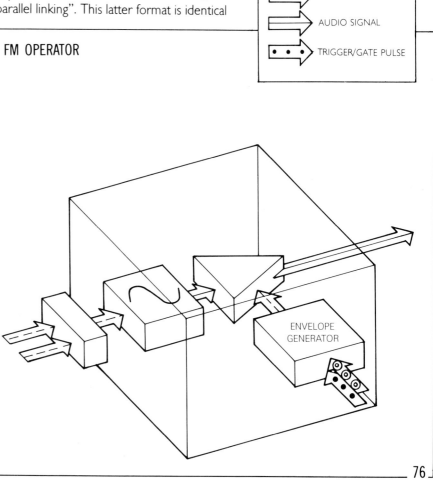

FM OPERATOR

ENVELOPE GENERATOR

76

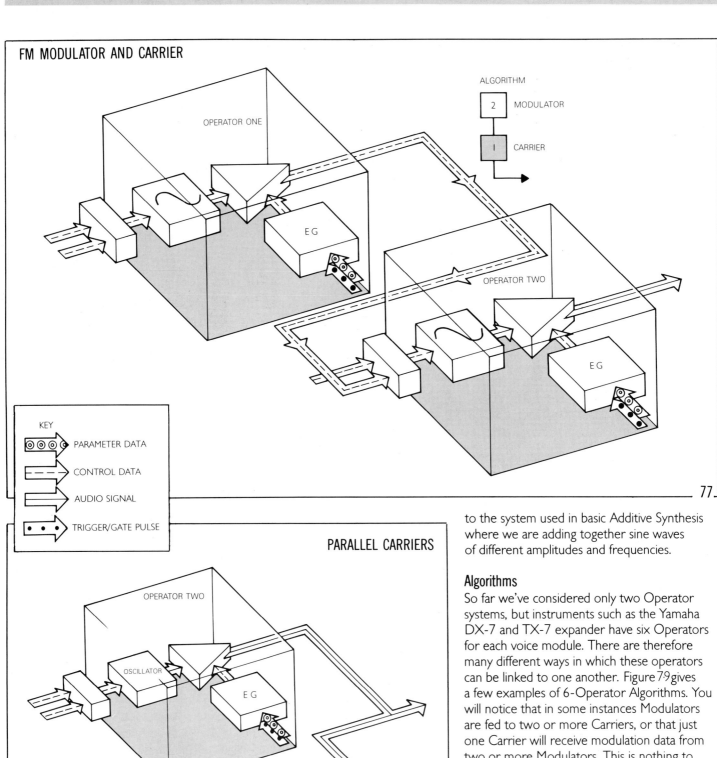

FM MODULATOR AND CARRIER

OPERATOR ONE

E G

ALGORITHM

2 — MODULATOR

I — CARRIER

OPERATOR TWO

E G

KEY

⊙⊙⊙ PARAMETER DATA

CONTROL DATA

AUDIO SIGNAL

• • • TRIGGER/GATE PULSE

PARALLEL CARRIERS

OPERATOR TWO

OSCILLATOR

E G

ALGORITHM

CARRIER 2   CARRIER 2

OPERATOR ONE

OSCILLATOR

E G

77

78

to the system used in basic Additive Synthesis where we are adding together sine waves of different amplitudes and frequencies.

Algorithms

So far we've considered only two Operator systems, but instruments such as the Yamaha DX-7 and TX-7 expander have six Operators for each voice module. There are therefore many different ways in which these operators can be linked to one another. Figure 79 gives a few examples of 6-Operator Algorithms. You will notice that in some instances Modulators are fed to two or more Carriers, or that just one Carrier will receive modulation data from two or more Modulators. This is nothing to worry about, though the latter can lead to some confusion when formulating the construction of a particular sound.

When you are creating a sound using an FM synthesizer, you need to choose a suitable Algorithm that will suit the sound goal. Firstly think "Should I be working horizontally or vertically?" Bear in mind that the more Carriers you have along the bottom in your Algorithm, the greater the layering possibilities, but this has to be traded off against the fact that the algorithm is of a "lower level", i.e. the fewer modulation stages you employ, the smaller the scope for making the Carriers harmonically rich. Consider a pipe organ sound. Pipe organs

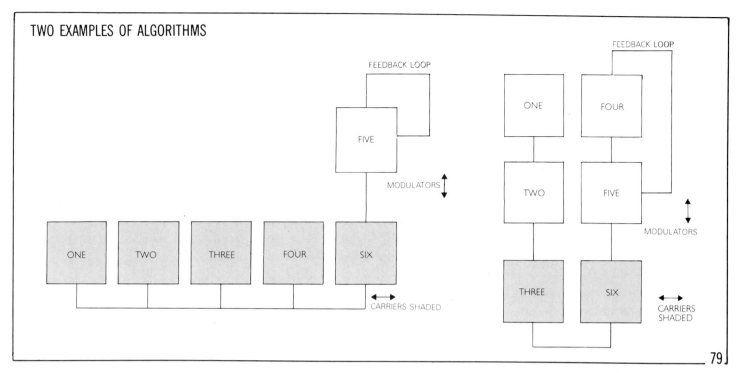

TWO EXAMPLES OF ALGORITHMS

FEEDBACK LOOP

FEEDBACK LOOP

FIVE

MODULATORS

ONE   TWO   THREE   FOUR   SIX

CARRIERS SHADED

ONE   FOUR

TWO   FIVE

MODULATORS

THREE   SIX

CARRIERS SHADED

79

have a leaning to combine several sets of pipes to produce parallel flute-like tones. A pipe organ proffers little timbral movement during the course of each note, so a parallel-linked Algorithm would make sense, though maybe you would need to introduce a few harmonically more complex timbres in order to simulate the more reedy stops. Contrast this to a saxophone type sound: this requires an extremely rich timbrally vibrant format, so a predominantly series-linked Algorithm would make a lot of sense.

Feedback

You may notice that virtually every Algorithm has a loop in it. This is known as the Feedback element, and what is happening is that a small amount of the output of an Operator is being routed back to its modulating input so that it is modulating itself. This results in an increase in the harmonic content of the Operator's output. There is a control facility that enables you to determine the amount of feedback in the loop. In certain instances this can be taken to such a degree that the Operator acts as a white noise source producing a random selection of pitches over the entire audio spectrum – so Feedback is a useful special effects tool. The Feedback element can also of course be set to zero, at which point the Operator behaves as any other.

FM – How it's Done

The modulation of one sine wave by another produces what are known as sidebands, or side frequencies above and below the frequency of the carrier. These sidebands are created at the

expense of the carrier, which is "distorted" by the modulator. The difference between the frequencies of the sidebands and the carrier is known as the frequency deviation.

These sidebands act as new harmonics to the tone produced and are the cause of the drastic metamorphosis of the original simple sine wave output.

Consider an instrument such as a DX-7. It has 6 Operators to each note and is 16-voice polyphonic, so it has a total of 96 sine wave generators and envelope generators contained within its metal/plastic casing. If you open up a DX-7 you will see that there is just a handful of chips (small black monolithic packages with up to 40 small silver legs) mounted on the main circuit board. To build an analogue sine wave generator requires several discrete bits of electronic hardware, so to create 96 such devices would not be practical.

So, as with additive synthesis, a digital technique is employed. All the data relating to sine waves is held in "lookup" tables. The sine waves are theoretically created in digital format, then manipulated by the processor in accordance with the envelope data and modulation indices.

Figure 80 illustrates a very simple example. Consider a sine wave of frequency fm modulating a carrier of frequency fc. The processor knows what is supposed to be happening and every few microseconds does a sum that takes the numeric value of the modulator and carrier, and produces a new number that is determined by the two frequencies and the modulation index. The formula for this equation is explained below.

This new number represents, in digital

format, the position of the modulated carrier at that specific instant in time. This number is then summed with the outputs for the other voices being played. The resulting waveform passes to the DAC which produces a voltage corresponding to the instantaneous level of the analogue waveform. A few microseconds later a completely new calculation will have been performed which results in the next step of the waveform.

Unless the steps are extremely small, you will nearly always notice some very slight buzzing noise when playing the low notes of an FM synth. This is due to the step approximation of the final waveform.

FM Mathematics

Unless you are of a particularly mathematical bent, you may wish to skip the rest of this section.

Firstly, it is necessary to understand how a waveform is defined mathematically. At this point we need to utilise the old schoolday favourite – angular velocity. A cycle of a waveform takes a certain period of time to complete, time 't' say. But the frequency isn't important when describing the shape of the waveform.

In order to define a particular waveform we have to divide the cycle into small steps and give a value for the position of the waveform at each step. If we aren't interested in time, how do we divide the waveform ?

Well, the best way to consider a sine wave is with reference to a circle. Figure 80. The line OA is a radius that moves round the circle once for every cycle of the waveform. It moves through 360 degrees. The height of the sine wave at a given instant corresponds to the point at which the radius line OR strikes the circle. So if we divide the horizontal centre line of our sine wave into 360 equal steps, the height of

the waveform at time 't' – H(t) is given by the formula

$$H(t) = sine\ x(t)$$

where $x(t)$ is the angle through which the radius has turned at time 't'. So, for example, take the position one quarter of the way through the cycle, i.e. when $x(t) = 90$ degrees (360/4). At this point $H(t) = sine\ 90$, i.e. $= 1$, this being the maximum value. And as you can see from the plot of the sine wave this is the case, because it is at a maximum value one quarter of the way through its cycle.

Dr. Chowning and Dr. Mathews evolved the following formula for the result of a carrier sine wave being acted upon by a modulating sine wave.

$$H(t) = sine\ (2 \times pi \times fc \times t) + \\ I\ sine\ [2 \times pi \times fm \times (t+P)]$$

It's not really as difficult as it appears.

$H(t)$ = the resulting height of the waveform at instant t

t = the point along the x-axis $(0 \leq t < 1)$

fc = the frequency of the carrier

fm = the frequency of the modulator

I = the modulation index, equal to the frequency deviation caused by the modulation divided by fm

P = the phase of the modulator.

If both waveforms started at exactly the same instant in time P would be zero. P is the phase difference between both waveforms $(-1 < P < 1)$.

This formula enables you to predict the shape of one operator modulating another – things get decidedly more difficult when three Operators are piled up as a series of substitutions are required.

The practical applications of FM Synthesis are discussed further in chapter 11.

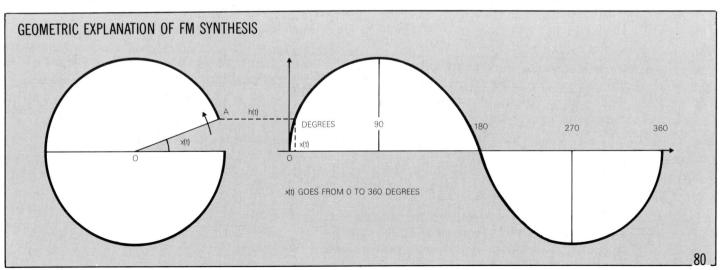

GEOMETRIC EXPLANATION OF FM SYNTHESIS

A   h(t)

x(t)

O

DEGREES   90   180   270   360

x(t)

O

x(t) GOES FROM 0 TO 360 DEGREES

80

PHASE DISTORTION SYNTHESIS

6

The Research and Development departments of the leading manufacturers throughout the world are constantly striving to evolve new synthesis techniques. The latest result, primarily from the labours of Casio, is that of PD Synthesis, which again employs digital manipulation to produce the desired voicings.

The aim of most research teams is to be able to create complex waveforms efficiently and in a manner that is easy for the musician to understand. Unfortunately, although FM Synthesis is fantastically powerful in the breadth of sounds it can realise, it is difficult for the musician to get to grips with, and to many the programming of an FM synthesizer is a somewhat hit and miss affair. The basic analogue VCO-VCF-VCA system is one that has obvious musical relationships, and most musicians find it easy to see why changing a certain parameter results in a particular change in the sound.

The Phase Distortion system attempts to offer a method of synthesis that is as flexible as FM, but as easy to understand as analogue subtractive synthesis. And to some extent the aims have been met.

Phase Distortion (PD) Synthesis

The actual use of PD Synthesis is relatively simple, but the explanation as to how it works involves some mathematics. Those who aren't particularly interested in the "technical hows?" should skip to the last paragraph under this heading.

In common with FM techniques, everything to do with PD is done digitally. We need now to utilise the concept of the phase angle.

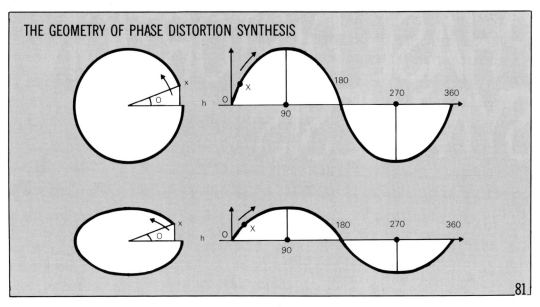

THE GEOMETRY OF PHASE DISTORTION SYNTHESIS

Look at Figure 81. Here we have a line drawn from the centre to a point X on the circumference (a radius OX). Point X travels round the circumference of the circle. The horizontal axis of the graph alongside is marked off in degrees, this corresponds to the angle 0 (the phase angle) which the radius makes with the horizontal. The vertical axis shows the position of the point X above or below the centre line. In fact this height can be calculated mathematically from the formula:

h = OX (the length) X sine O

OX can be considered as unity ("1"). If we were now to plot the position of X for different angles O we would in fact get the shape of a sine wave, and one cycle of the waveform would correspond to a 360 degrees variation in the phase angle.

If instead of a circle we had a slightly different shape (b), the resulting waveform would of course be different. To define such a shape we need only specify a series of angles (0) and corresponding radii (OX).

Now we've established what a phase angle is and does, consider figure 82a, which shows a sinusoidally varying waveform. The horizontal axis is time. To make things clear, we'll start at point Z, and say that this corresponds to phase angle zero. Figure 82b shows the phase angle 0 up the vertical axis also plotted against time, and as you can see it is a straight line – this is because the phase angle of the sine wave changes at a constant speed.

What would happen, though, if we were to alter the rate of change of the phase angle, i.e. use something other than a straight line. Figure 83 shows what would happen if the phase angle changed more quickly over the first 180 degrees, then slowed down over the second part of the cycle. You can see that the sine wave has been distorted and now takes a somewhat different shape.

By making the phase angle rate changes even more dramatic we can create all manner of different waveforms. Remember the overall time that the phase angle takes to complete its 360 degree cycle must remain constant, otherwise the pitch will change.

To sum up, we have a simple mechanism for creating a plethora of different waveforms by means of distorting the shape of a sine wave (by varying the rate at which the phase angle changes). So in terms of the actual digital circuitry required, the sine wave is stored in "look-up" tables, and all that is required is to generate a string of numbers that stipulate the continually variable 'distortion' that is needed to produce the desired effect.

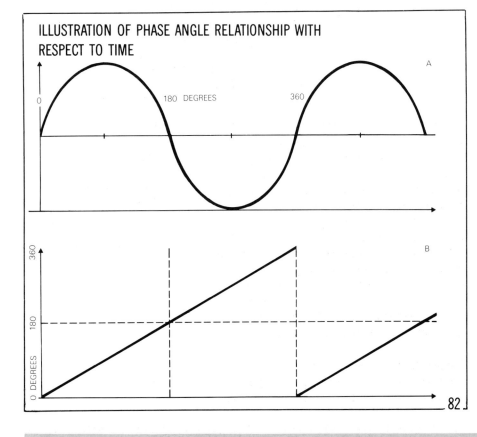

ILLUSTRATION OF PHASE ANGLE RELATIONSHIP WITH RESPECT TO TIME

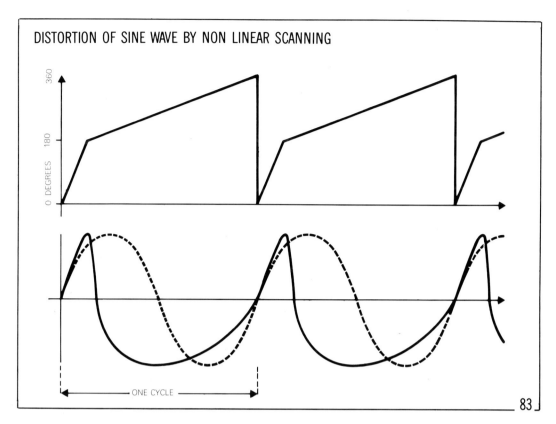

DISTORTION OF SINE WAVE BY NON LINEAR SCANNING

360

180

0 DEGREES

ONE CYCLE

83

A PD Voice Module

As it was the Casio Computer Co. Ltd. which developed this system, it makes sense to discuss PD Synthesis with respect to one of the Casio products. The CZ-101 and the larger CZ-1000 are very similar in their working formats, so we will base our discussions on these two machines. As with most other forms of synthesis, it is the voice module that features the specific revolutionary techniques. The format of the rest of the instrument – controller, performance controls etc, – can be covered under a section relevant to all synthesizers.

The block diagram of a typical PD Synthesizer voice module is shown in figure 84. You will notice that it bears a close similarity to the VCO-VCF-VCA subtractive system, and it is probably useful to consider it in this manner. The fundamentals as discussed above, however, are quite different.

The CZ instruments have two identical 'lines' of oscillator, filter, and amplifer, and each element has its own envelope generator. The pitch of the two oscillators can be detuned in order to provide beating effects, thus enhancing the timbral depth of the sound.

The Digitally Controlled Oscillator (DCO)
On the face of it, this is a very similar device to the conventional DCO. Pitch data is forwarded by the central processor to the voice module and an apparent oscillating waveform is

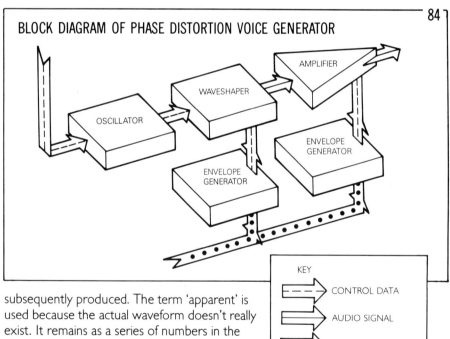

BLOCK DIAGRAM OF PHASE DISTORTION VOICE GENERATOR

84

AMPLIFIER

WAVESHAPER

OSCILLATOR

ENVELOPE GENERATOR

ENVELOPE GENERATOR

KEY

CONTROL DATA

AUDIO SIGNAL

TRIGGER/GATE PULSE

subsequently produced. The term 'apparent' is used because the actual waveform doesn't really exist. It remains as a series of numbers in the circuitry of the instrument, but the workings are far easier to understand this way.

The DCO offers a range of preset waveforms – all distorted from the original sine wave, and the envelope generator facilitates the aperiodic variation of pitch with time – i.e. swooping, auto-glide etc. The CZ series of instruments offers sawtooth, square and pulse waves; a couple of more elaborate waveshapes; and three highly resonant waveforms.

The Digitally Controlled Wave (DCW)
This stage equates to the voltage controlled filter of the subtractive synthesizer, except that

with a PD instrument there is no filter.

The DCW envelope is used to vary the distortion of the wave over the course of its duration; thus the harmonic spectrum of the sound can be totally varied by this envelope. As shown in figure 85 the harmonic content can be made to rise and fall with the shape of the envelope. When envelope modulation is applied, the output of the DCO always originates as a sine wave and 'distorts' into the selected waveform as it reaches a peak. The reverse happens during the decay/release phase.

If a resonant output from the DCO is used, then the application of the envelope generator causes the resulting waveform to become increasingly resonant during the attack phase. This is very similar to the effect encountered when using analogue filters.

A Key Follow facility is also provided. This enables the actual shape of the waveform produced to vary depending on what note is played on the controller. Generally, the higher the note, the closer the waveform approaches a sine wave (i.e. the lesser the harmonic content). Figure 86 shows the effect on a sawtooth wave of various degrees of Key Follow.

The Digitally Controlled Amplifier (DCA)

The DCA is a very close relative of the VCA. It attenuates and amplifies the signal from the DCW in response to the envelope applied to it. Like the DCW, it has a Key Follow facility, but this time the higher the note played, the shorter the overall length of the envelope. This facility was incorporated by Roland in some of their analogue synthesizers. Essentially its purpose is to simulate the acoustic inertia of certain instruments. For example the length of a plucked cello note is less, the higher the note played. The Key Follow facility enables the user to copy this trait.

The outputs of both lines of the voice module are then combined to form the final output for that voice.

Envelope Generators (PDEGs)

The traditional ADSR envelope is not really flexible enough for the PD synthesizer. The envelope is the all important factor in this kind of system, so in the case of the Casio CZ series, a more versatile Rate-Level Envelope Generator (RLEG) is used (see figure 87).

There are up to 8 level stages, with intermediate rate times.

In addition, there are two further parameters that may be specified – SUSTAIN and END. Sustain stipulates which of the eight stages should be the sustain level, and End is used to state which Level is the last – i.e. you might want to use only the first four stages of the envelope, so Level 4 would be set to END, thus negating the need to program any of the subsequent Rates and Levels. Figure 87 shows a particularly complex envelope that it is possible to create using this system, there being two 'Attacks', before the Sustain Level, and a third upon release of the key.

As stated, there are separate envelopes for each DCO, DCW and DCA. But again it should be remembered that the envelope generator is not real in the analogue way. It exists as a train of numbers within the instrument's digital circuitry, and these numbers act on the numbers that represent the basic waveshape to produce the final result.

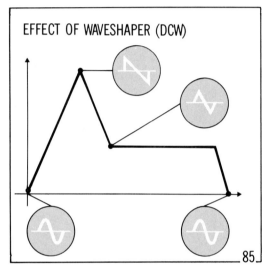

EFFECT OF WAVESHAPER (DCW)

85

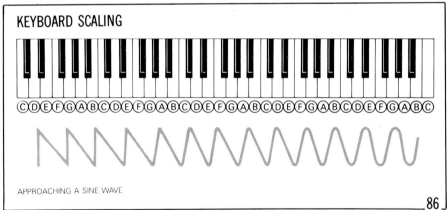

KEYBOARD SCALING

C D E F G A B C D E F G A B C D E F G A B C D E F G A B C D E F G A B C

APPROACHING A SINE WAVE

86

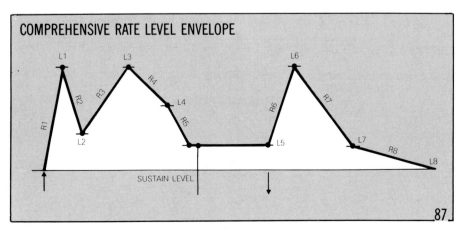

COMPREHENSIVE RATE LEVEL ENVELOPE

SUSTAIN LEVEL

87

MORE SYNTHESIS TECHNIQUES

7

Geometric Synthesis

Geometric Synthesis is a relatively straightforward method of creating desired sounds; however it can be 'thirsty' in terms of the memory capacity required within the instrument. In the New Synthesizer digital technology, memory is the all important criterion, basically because memory costs money.

What is a memory ? Quite simply it is a device which enables you to store information. This information can be retrieved at a later date. There are all manner of different kinds of memory, and most of these are explained on p. 93. Here we are dealing with internal electronic memory. That is to say circuits that hold the information required to shape the waveform. The greater the memory capacity, the more faithfully a sound can be synthesized.

Geometric Synthesis involves dividing the waveform of a sound into steps, typically 40,000+ per second, and specifying the value of a step at each step in time. Now this is a digital technique so it is necessary to represent the actual position of the waveform at any instant by a digital number (see figure 88). Ideally, as most microprocessors utilise 8 bits of information (8 binary digits to represent a number), then we can specify the position of the waveform to an accuracy of 1:256. This is because an 8-bit number can be anything from zero (00000000) to 256 (11111111) – see figure 88.

So if we wanted to simulate a simple sine wave tone lasting 2 seconds using geometric synthesis, we would need to store at least 80,000 8-bit numbers – 80K of memory. Of course this is ridiculous, because there are many better ways to create a sine wave, and this is very memory-inefficient because, as the sine wave is constantly repeating itself during the 2 second period, you are simply storing the same pattern of numbers over and over. If we want the amplitude to change over this period, we simply decrease the height of the step points accordingly, and, in fact, the sound can thus be

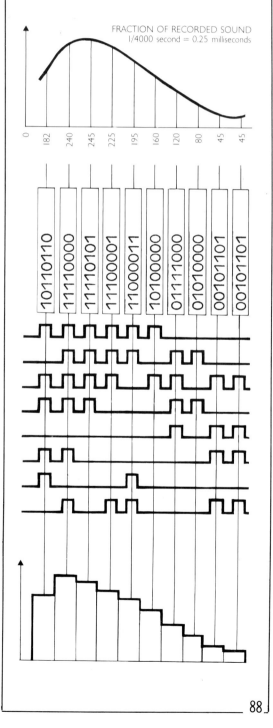

TRANSLATION OF ANALOGUE TO DIGITAL

FRACTION OF RECORDED SOUND
1/4000 second = 0.25 milliseconds

0 182 240 245 225 195 160 120 80 45 45

10110110 11110000 11110101 11100001 11000011 10100000 01111000 01010000 00101101 00101101

1 A segment of sound to be digitized. The numbers indicate the amplitude of the waveform at incremental 'timesteps'. The amplitude can be defined in steps from 0 to 255 (0 to 100%).

2 The amplitudes are converted to binary numbers as shown. 8-bits (digits) are required to give this resolution. Each 8-bit number is known as a byte.

3 Each bit is 'carried' by one of eight parallel lines — one for each binary digit.

4 Digital representation of original signal. For finer resolution the number of steps per second can be increased.

88

made to fade out completely over its duration.

Geometric synthesis enables us to specify any wave-train over the duration of the note so we can create an amazingly complex sound if we know how and where to specify the points.

Once a table of the step values is created, it is possible to feed it to all the voices for polyphonic use. The way in which the pitch is varied is by shortening or decreasing the step time for each segment of the waveform. This is all done under the auspices of the central processor. Note that this variation in the step length also leads to the shortening and lengthening of the duration of the notes at the top and bottom ends of the keyboard respectively.

Timbre and Amplitude can be varied over the duration of the note. Again all the changes have to be written into the number chain, which may not be easy in some contexts.

There are more simple forms of geometric synthesis that use a series of numbers to represent just the fixed shape of a cyclic waveform. To change amplitude and timbre with time requires conventional analogue filter and amplifier circuitry.

It is important to realise that the smaller the time steps and the greater the number of possible values that the position of the waveform can have at any one instant in time, the better the resolution of the sound that you are trying to synthesise, and the less the distortion. It all boils down to how much memory has been made available. See also Digital Waveform Oscillators (see p.71).

Consonant-Vowel Synthesis

One very useful variant on the technology of geometric synthesis is that of Consonant-Vowel (C-V, not to be confused with CV, which refers to control voltage) Synthesis. This is a low cost technique that is memory efficient yet still enables the user to vary both amplitude and timbre over the period of the note.

The fundamental principle on which the system works, and in fact from which it is named, comes from the way in which the human voice articulates when speaking. Consider what happens when we say the word "to". The sound we make can be broken down into two parts, "t" and "ooo". The former is known as the consonant phase, and the latter the vowel. And by joining the two sounds we get the complete word (see figure 89).

Basically that is how C-V Synthesis operates. Two sounds are given different pitch, amplitude, and timbral characteristics, then run into one another to create a composite sound.

The system can best be explained by

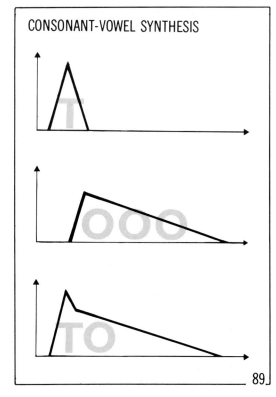

CONSONANT-VOWEL SYNTHESIS

89

referring to figure 90, which shows the block diagram of the system's voice module. The controller data is sent to both the consonant and vowel generators. These produce waveforms geometrically. Each waveform is then fed to a voltage controlled amplifier (or digital equivalent) to have its amplitude shaped by an envelope generator. There the timbre of both tones remains constant over their duration. Timbral movement is created when the two phases are mixed, and such movement is dictated by the shape of the two envelopes.

One of the earliest examples of the use of this consonant vowel system was with the original electric organs, which featured harmonic percussion. Here the consonant phase was a short percussive stab of a particular harmonic which accentuated the 'arrival' of the main body of the note.

Casio were more recently the prime advocates of this method of simulating and synthesising sounds, although they don't actually use the system in their new generation of synthesizers. When formulating the preset sounds of their instruments, two separate sounds would be created and mixed in order to simulate a wide range of acoustic voicings. For example, a piano sound would have a bright percussive consonant phase, then mellow as the second part of the sound took over.

The Consonant-Vowel system does not have to operate in the strict sense of producing a hard percussive sound, then a more rounded sustained tone. The parameters of the system can be reversed; or two completely diverse sounds in different registers can be utilised. Any

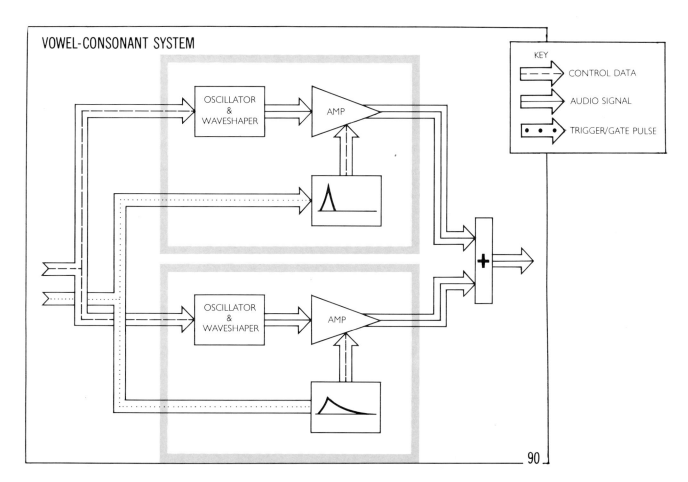

VOWEL-CONSONANT SYSTEM

OSCILLATOR & WAVESHAPER

AMP

KEY

CONTROL DATA

AUDIO SIGNAL

TRIGGER/GATE PULSE

OSCILLATOR & WAVESHAPER

AMP

+

90

pair of signals can be used to create the composite sound – the key to the system is that the two envelope generators cause a cross fade between the two sounds and this is the device that produces the timbral movement.

C-V Synthesis has found itself a niche in the personal computer field. This is primarily as a result of a company (Mountain Computer Inc.) developing a synthesizer voice card that plugs into one of the expansion ports of an Apple Computer. The Mountain voice card gives the computer user access to a high powered C-V Synthesis system, enabling very precise definition of waveforms and envelopes.

Several companies such as Syntauri Inc. and Passport Designs have taken the Mountain card and developed comprehensive software and hardware to turn the Apple + Mountain system into an easy-to-use performance and studio orientated instrument.

Sampling

Sampling is the synthesizer "buzz-word" of the Eighties, and on the face of it seems to offer more to the electronic musician than any other form of synthesis (that is if sampling can be considered a form of synthesis).

The concept is a fairly simple one, although its implementation is less so. Sampling in its crudest form is akin to getting a tape recorder

and recording a sound, then playing the tape back at different speeds in order to pitch the sound at different frequencies. For example, if we took a recording of an oboe playing an A-440 then played it back at half speed, we would hear an A-220 oboe note (one octave down); play it back at twice the speed, and we get an A-880 (an octave up). So by playing the note back at different intermediary rates we can get pitches that fall on any frequency in between.

Some early examples of sampling instruments were the Chamberlain and its direct descendant the Mellotron, which appeared in the early Sixties. These keyboard based instruments are, however, more correctly termed Replay machines than samplers. They utilised actual tape recordings of real instruments; there was a magnetic tape replay head situated under each key and when the note was played the tape would be drawn over the head and the recorded sound would be heard. Thus you could produce any previously recorded sound using one of these instruments, and because every key had its own piece of tape, you could have all manner of different tones available from the one keyboard. Not only were these devices used for musical applications, with racks of tape recordings of acoustic instruments, but also this kind of instrument was ideal for sound effects work. For example, one key might have waves on it, the next a fog horn, another some sea-gulls,

REPLAYING

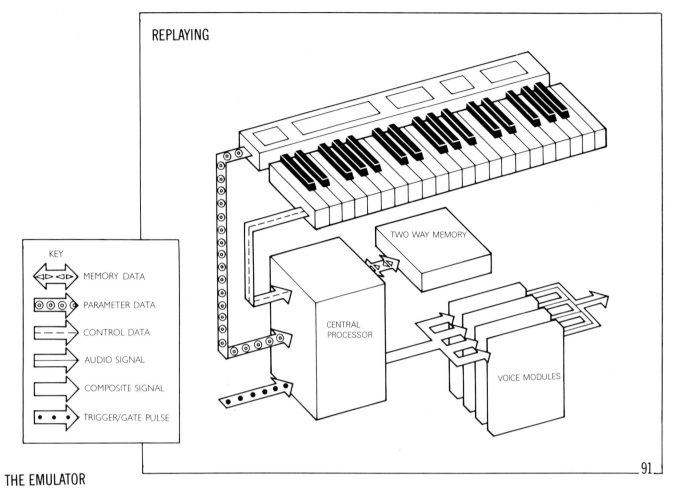

KEY

MEMORY DATA

PARAMETER DATA

CONTROL DATA

AUDIO SIGNAL

COMPOSITE SIGNAL

TRIGGER/GATE PULSE

TWO WAY MEMORY

CENTRAL PROCESSOR

VOICE MODULES

91

THE EMULATOR

THE ENSONIQ MIRAGE

etc. So it would be possible to create a composite set of special effects using this replay system.

Although the replay system is good, sampling enables the user to load his own sounds into the instrument's digital memory banks. The block diagram of the system is shown in figure 91. A sound is sampled and turned into a train of digital numbers via an ADC (analogue to digital convertor).

Two things determine the quality of the sampled sound:

1 Sampling rate. The usable band width of the resultant signal is just under a half the sample rate. So, as the audible frequency spectrum extends above 12,000 Hz, to get good quality results the sound needs to be sampled at around 30,000 cycles per second, that is to say every thirty thousandth of a second the waveform produced by the source is examined and a number given for representing its value. A one second sound can thus be efficiently represented by a string of 30,000 numbers.

2 The resolution. If we are using an 8-bit system we can express each step with a binary number whose decimal equivalent can be anywhere between 0 and 255 – a resolution of 1:256. This gives a fairly acceptable sound, but when listening to lower frequencies it is possible to detect a 'quantization effect', i.e. you can detect that the waveform is stepping between levels. The more upmarket forms of sampler use 12-bit, or even 16-bit, binary numbers, which have a resolution of 1:4096, and 1:65,536 respectively.

So, we've sampled our sound, and the number is then stored in the computer's volatile wavetable memory.

When a note is played, the central processor looks to see which note is free, then makes the set of numbers stored in the wavetable available to that voice. The voice under command of the central processor then sends the binary numbers to a DAC (digital to analogue convertor) and then on to the output of the instrument.

The pitch of a note is determined by the rate at which the numbers are fed to the ensuing DAC. For example, if our sample is of the A-440 oboe note, and the corresponding A Key is played, then the central processor will send out 30,000 pulses every second and we hear the original sound. If the A above is played, 60,000 pulses are sent out per second, and the pitch goes up an octave. But obviously, because the clock is twice the speed, the sample comes to its end in half the time.

Polyphonic sampling is a simple matter of

having a more powerful processor that can efficiently handle the multiple number manipulation.

The main advantage of sampling is that you can recreate any sound and transpose it into any key. It should be made clear that we aren't just sampling a waveform, we are sampling a full sound. So we can capture every nuance of the original. If, for example, we were to sample the sound of a note on an acoustic piano, we would capture the percussive attack, the sympathetic resonance of the other strings, the decay phase, etc. We wouldn't have simply derived a waveform that the piano makes at one particular instant in time. We would have sampled the complete note, and every time the voice is retriggered we would always hear that sound from the start.

But sampling also has three problems, all of which are to some degree surmountable.

1 The length of the sample
2 The resonant distortion of the sample
3 The lack of articulation

1) Memory space

Sampling is an expensive business because a lot of memory is required, and the processor has to be very powerful and fast in order to handle all the operation. Consider the sound of a single sustained piano note – it can take over 10 seconds to die away. This would require 300K (300,000 8- or 12-digit binary numbers) of memory, which is a considerable amount. And, in addition, what happens if we want to hold an oboe voice for a period longer than the time over which the sample was taken, will the sound just cut out? Yes, like the Mellotron when it came to the end of the piece of tape it was replaying.

One way around this is to loop the signal. Look at figure 92 which represents our oboe note. The envelope of the sample rises quickly and then sustains at a maximum level until the note finishes and the amplitude dies away fairly rapidly. If we play the sample, we would initially be able to recreate only this envelope. But if we

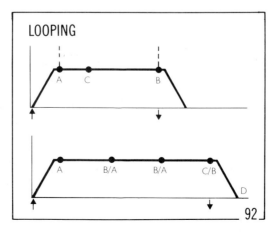

LOOPING

92

specify a portion in the middle of the sample where the envelope and harmonic content of the sound is virtually constant, and identify these points, then so long as the respective note on the sampling instrument's keyboard is held down, the processor will cause the output train of numbers to loop round. And only when the key has been released will the final phase of the sample be replayed.

Again this can be shown more clearly if the sample was of someone saying "black . . and . . white". The two 'flags' identifying the section to be looped could be positioned either side of the ". . and . .", so when a key is pressed and held, we would hear "black . . and . . and . . and . . and . ." until the key were to be released then the last part of the sample ". . white" would be heard. Retriggering the same note would lead to something like "bl . . bl . . bl . . bl . . bl . . black" the amount of the first word depending on how long the note is held.

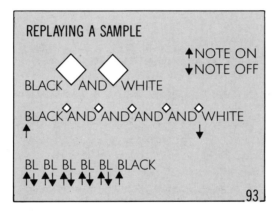

2) Resonance and Envelope Distortion

Every body that can vibrate (oscillate) has a resonant frequency, i.e. one at which it finds it easier to oscillate at more than at any other (see p.13). A violincello might have a resonant frequency of say 100Hz, so any component of the note that falls nearby will tend to sound more prominent. The human voice has two resonant frequencies and these give rise to its individual characteristic. The resonant frequency(s) is fixed for any sound. But when we sample a sound and then play it back in different keys, we are also transposing the resonant frequency(s) and thus changing the very character of the sound. We are of course also changing the time span of the envelope. A sound transposed up an octave will last half the time; this effect is to some extent related to the way in which acoustic instruments behave, but not to anywhere near the severity.

To get around this problem the keyboard is split up into several sections and a different sample taken for each section. In this way the sample becomes less corrupted by the frequency multiplication, and the sound less compacted by the increase in pitch.

3) Articulation

To many, the biggest problem with a sampling instrument is the inability to articulate the sound. That is to say, when you press a note the only control you have over the ensuing sound is its duration (determined by how long you hold down the key) and in some cases pitchbend – the position of the pitchbend wheel dictating the rate at which the sample is played back and hence its pitch.

More recently however, we've seen hybrid instruments that feature both sampling systems and more conventional analogue circuitry – filters, LFOs, and envelopes etc. The sample can then be processed by these facilities to further enhance the sound output. Now this type of analogue circuitry facilitates the real time articulation of the sound, especially if the instrument is equipped with a dynamic controller, i.e. a velocity and/or pressure sensitive keyboard. We now have a way to inject expression into our erstwhile stolid sample. This makes sampling a much more attractive proposition to the musician.

CONTROLS & CONTROLLERS TECHNIQUES 8

We have already described the basic role of the controller and control panel (see p. 28 and 29), and have gleaned that the controller feeds the musical requirements to the central processor which passes them on to the voices, and the control panel determines how this controller data will be handled when it reaches the voice modules.

But now having dealt with the workings of the various categories of voice modules, we can take a closer look at the various control mechanisms and how they are used to maximum efficiency.

The Keyboard

Keyboards are in many cases just a series of electronic switches. A synthesizer is a creative tool and its design is perfect for injecting all manner of animation into its sound. An electric organ, on the other hand offers little or no leeway to inject feel into individual notes, as its keyboard offers only a choice between a particular note being on or off. The keyboard on many of today's synthesizers can provide much more.

Size
Generally, monophonic synthesizers require at least a 3-octave keyboard, though a 3-1/2 octave C (to G) span is accepted as the best. If you are using a polyphonic synthesizer as an additional keyboard to another polyphonic instrument, and you will be playing only single hand chord clusters, then a 4-octave keyboard (C to C is best) will suffice. But if you intend to play the instrument with both hands on the keyboard, a 5-octave (C to C) keyboard is really essential, especially if you intend to split the keyboard (see p.80).

There is an increasingly strong trend towards touch sensitive (sometimes called touch responsive) keyboards. This is because they are infinitely more versatile and expressive than the simple "on/off-switch" keyboard.

There are two main types of touch sensitivity: velocity, and pressure. One doesn't negate the other, and in fact many instruments offer both facilities.

Velocity Sensitivity
Here a control signal is generated which is directly proportional to the speed at which the key is depressed. This requires a relatively simple mechanism for each key; viz. there are two contacts instead of one. When the key is depressed one contact is made, then as the key reaches the end of its travel a second closes. The central processor is informed of both 'makings' and automatically generates a control signal which reflects the velocity with which the key was played.

With an analogue synthesizer this velocity control signal generally takes the final form of a control voltage, while digital machines will naturally cause a digital signal to be induced.

Generally speaking, velocity sensitivity is a polyphonic mechanism (if you are employing a polyphonic instrument.) This is to say that each note in a chord will have its own velocity signal independently routed to the respective voice module.

Pressure Sensitivity
This is often known as After or Second touch, and involves the generation of a control signal after the key has been depressed. A sensor strip is set along the underside of the actual keyboard, and when a key is depressed it comes to rest on this strip. By applying further pressure, the strip is compressed and a control signal is induced. The harder the key is held down the greater the control signal.

By virtue of its design, the pressure sensing mechanism is generally a monophonic facility; i.e. the resulting control signal is sent to all the voice modules.

'X' and 'Y' Movements
Some more esoteric instruments feature other forms of control mechanisms. These are generally to be found on hybrid machines, and not on mass market synthesizers, because they are very expensive to manufacture.

The 'X'-movement simply generates a

control signal by physically moving the played key to the left or right. The actual scale of the movement is very slight – a matter of a few millimetres, but it is still quite a controllable facility.

Yamaha pioneered this form of touch sensitive keyboard and used it on several of their electronic organs to introduce vibrato. The movement required was akin to that of a violinist when he rocks back and forth on the string.

The 'Y' movement is an extremely rare beast. It involves the movement of the key back into the instrument, so to activate it you would hold down a note then push the key forward. The most obvious use for this mechanism would be for pitchbending (raising the pitch) or opening and closing the filter, or equivalent.

Applications

The most established and traditional of all keyboard instruments is the pianoforte. It gets its name from "piano e forte" soft and loud. And that's what has led to the demand for touch sensitive keyboards. The majority of today's keyboard players will have learnt on a piano, and consequently they will have developed a touch technique enabling them to play expressively – the harder the note is hit, the louder it will sound.

There is a correlation between this and the velocity sensitive keyboard. The harder you hit the note, the faster it travels and thus the greater the induced control signal. So a

synthesizer equipped with a velocity sensing keyboard can begin to equate to the action of the acoustic piano.

The keyboards of most synthesizers, however, are plastic and sprung. An acoustic instrument has a weighted keyboard, and is generally made of wood. Consequently it has a greater inertia and requires the player to have stronger fingers. The acoustic pianist will therefore find it easier to go to the synthesizer's keyboard than a person used to a synthesizer keyboard will find the action of an acoustic piano. There is, however, an increasing trend towards the use of heavier weighted keys for keyboard controllers. These keyboards are in fact still sprung, but weights are attached to the underside of every key to give it a more solid feel. It is easier to utilise the velocity sensing facilities with this kind of keyboard.

Naturally, this resultant signal can be used to control parameters other than just volume. In fact the harder you hit an acoustic piano key the brighter the sound – so some part of the signal can be routed so as to relate the harmonic content to the velocity at which the key is played. Few, if any, instruments route the key velocity signal to the pitch of the voice module as this is not a particularly relevant option.

Pressure sensitivity is primarily used for introducing vibrato – i.e. periodic pitch modulation. A note is played and held. Then, when you want to animate the sound, a degree of extra pressure is applied to the key which introduces the modulation.

Other secondary applications of pressure sensitivity include: increase in brightness; pitchbend; periodic timbral modulation.

Keyboard Splits

A split keyboard is not a broken one. We define a split keyboard as being divided into two (sometimes three) sections with one set of voice modules, which are producing one sound assigned to the upper keys, and another set of voices set up to produce a different sound assigned to the lower keys. Thus we could have, say, a piano-like sound for the bottom accompaniment chords and perhaps a flute voicing for the melody line. The point at which the transition takes place is known as the split point. Generally, only the more expensive synthesizers offer this facility; in some instances the split will be fixed, in others the split is variable and can be set by the player.

With technology constantly changing, two types of split have evolved. The above example of the piano and flute voicings assigned to the Lower and Upper sections of the keyboard is known as a "hard split". Either side of the split

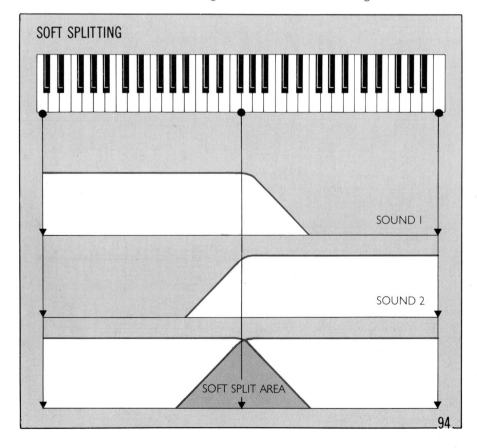

SOFT SPLITTING

SOUND 1

SOUND 2

SOFT SPLIT AREA

94

point, one key will produce one sound and the next a different one. A second type of split is known as the "soft split", and here the two sounds fade into one another. See figure 94.

What's the point of a soft split ? Well, consider our friend the acoustic piano. The actual character of the instrument changes as you play up and down the keyboard. At the top end the sound is bright and thin, whereas towards the bottom end of the keyboard the timbre becomes mellower and the sound fuller. So, by setting up both sets of voices to produce similar sounds, but with the lower register given a more mellow timbre, and the upper a brighter quality, the qualities of an acoustic piano can be realised better as the soft split will not easily be noticed.

Sampling keyboards, as discussed in the previous section, may have several different split points with samples of sounds in different registers assigned to each. This is to maintain the authenticity of the voicing over the entire span of the keyboard.

Layering, Doubling, or Stacking

Layering is achieved when two or more voice modules are assigned to the keys being played. The sounds produced by each module would in most instances be different. This would equate to a hybrid consonant/vowel type of synthesis, such that two completely different signals could be layered on top of one another to realise a third, more complex and interesting, sound.

Under normal conditions, a synthesizer will only facilitate two voice modules being doubled up. This, of course, halves the polyphonic capabilities of the instrument (if you use an 8-voice synth in Double mode, you therefore reduce it to a 4-voice).

The most exciting development in this field is the Yamaha TX-816 system. This is a sound generator unit consisting of eight independent sets of 16-voice polyphonic FM voice modules. See figure 95. When a note is played on the controller keyboard, one voice from each of the eight voice modules sounds. So you can have eight layered voices contributing a different quality to the overall sound. For example, you might want to synthesize various types of pipe organ – each of the eight units could form a different category of pipe, and thus with all eight layered up, you would produce a Full Organ voicing. And, of course, this system is still 16-note polyphonic.

Stacking is when ALL the voices of an otherwise polyphonic instrument are triggered when a single note is played – i.e. the synthesizer becomes monophonic. A good example of an instrument that can employ this

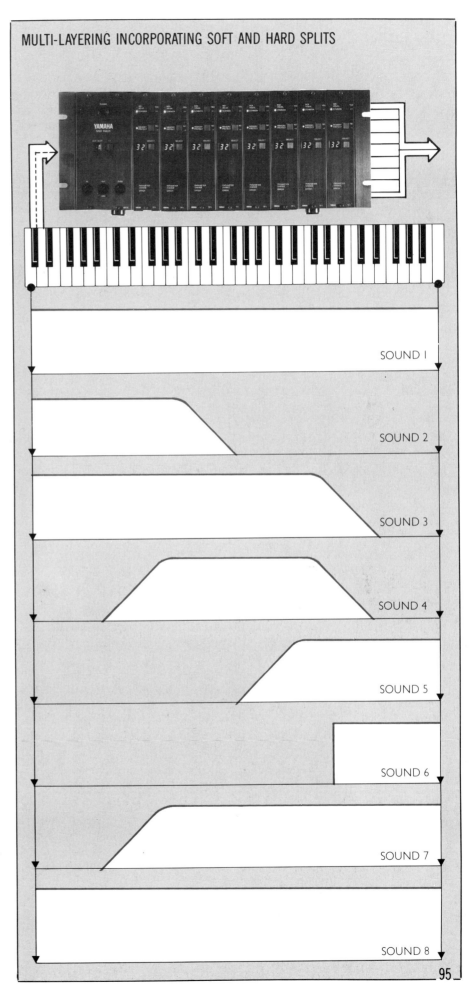

MULTI-LAYERING INCORPORATING SOFT AND HARD SPLITS

SOUND 1
SOUND 2
SOUND 3
SOUND 4
SOUND 5
SOUND 6
SOUND 7
SOUND 8

95

WHEELS:▶
The two performance control wheels are located at the left end of the instrument. The pitchbender has a centre-dente so it can be moved both up and down, and then be returned to a central position to restore correct tuning.

facility is Sequential's (a US manufacturer formerly known as Sequential Circuits Inc.) Multitrak. Each of the instrument's six voice modules can be programmed to give a different sound, and when in stack mode the instrument becomes monophonic with all six voices contributing to a single composite sound.

Performance Controls

A performance control is a mechanism that allows a synthesizer player to manually change a certain parameter of a sound while the sound is actually being heard.

Performance controls are possibly the most important aspect of electronic music synthesis. They enable the player to inject expression, feeling, and articulation into whatever he is playing.

In the late Sixties, when the synthesizer was just starting to make its mark, the instrument was criticised for being too clinical and machine-like. The critics should have taken a closer look at the instrument, however, because the performance controls that were featured on most instruments gave it a truly expressive power, far more so than the electronic organ, or even many acoustic instruments.

With the performance control you can "get inside" each and every note. It is possible to work between notes, instead of being fixed to strict harmonic intervals.

Any control that is twiddled or moved while a note is sounding can be termed a performance control, but there are two main elements that most musicians want to vary in order to add extra expression to the music being played – pitchbend and vibrato. Following the trend set by Dr. Moog with his Minimoog, controls that could be used to introduce these two effects were enlarged and moved away from the congestion of all the other controls to a position that the player could easily find – usually to a flat panel just to the left of the keyboard.

Pitchbend

The function of the "pitchbender" control is to smoothly vary the pitch of a note by no more than one octave (up or down). The control should easily return to its initial central position, so that when the instrument is not in use the synthesizer reverts to normal tuning.

Pitchbender technique owes a lot to the style of the electric guitarist. In fact the term "bending" a note is derived from the way in which extra tension is applied by bending a string out of shape to raise the pitch.

Modulation

The second performance control is needed to introduce modulation to a note. Unlike pitchbending, this is a one-way operation; i.e. you start with no performance modulation, then add the effect as necessary. A classic example of performance modulation can be heard when listening to a violinist. He will usually introduce vibrato to a long sustained note to add a degree of animation.

The Wheels

The Minimoog was a classic musical instrument. Bob Moog and his team got it just right when they designed this synthesizer. They were working in a vacuum, there being no other instruments around to copy, but they came up with a superb piece of design engineering (even if the tuning was originally a little suspect). One facet of the early machine was the performance controls – wheels – and although there have been many variations and different mechanisms mooted, the wheels have survived and are undoubtedly the most popular of all the performance controls.

There are two wheels of which only a small arc protrudes above the instrument's chassis – see above. They are rather like enormous wheel edge-wheel controls. The pitchbend has what is known as a "centre-dente". This is a notch cut into the wheel enabling it to be returned to its initial position every time after use. The centre-dente has to work perfectly; the slightest inaccuracy in the position to which it returns will result in the synthesizer being put out of tune. Pitchbend is a monophonic effect. When the control is used, all the notes will shift in pitch and keep their same harmonic relationship to one another.

Pitchbending is an art. You need to be able to bend a note exactly the amount you want without overshooting. Another useful way in which to use the pitchbend control is to start with the note out of tune and pull it back into tune.

The modulation wheel generally sits to the right of the pitchbender so that it is possible to move both controls simultaneously with one hand. This control is primarily used to introduce vibrato or trill (sine or square wave pitch modulation) to the note being played. Many synthesizers offer various extra routing facilities, but musically the vibrato/trill option is the most important. The modulation wheel determines how much LFO signal is routed to the pitch control of the oscillators.

This form of performance modulation is generally used towards the end of a note in much the same way as a violinist adds vibrato. The control mechanism is generally left at zero, and brief bursts of modulation added. As there is no spring return mechanism this wheel can be left in any position, thus providing a constant amount of modulation.

STRIPS:▶
The metallic strip shown here on YAMAHA KX-5 keyboard controller. Touching the centre of the strip causes no change in pitch, whilst pressure either side of this centre point will raise or lower the pitch proportionally.

BENDERS:▲
This is a lever that can be moved to the left or right to lower or raise the pitch. The lever is centre sprung and resets to a central position when released.

JOYSTICK:▼
A left/right movement of the joystick will lower/raise the pitch, whilst up/down movement will introduce LFP modulation.

Other Performance control mechanisms

● Levers. These are similar in principle to the wheels. They consist of two vertically mounted levers, one for pitchbend, the other for modulation, see right. However, both are sprung so that they return to their central position on release. For the pitchbender this is fine, but the modulation cannot be left a certain amount. Lever mechanisms are primarily used on machines produced by Oberheim Electronics.

● Ribbons. This mechanism is rarely seen now. It consists of a strip of metal (sometimes covered in felt) (see right). The pitch of the note varies depending on where you touch the strip, thus pitchbend can be affected by sliding your finger from a central dead' position until you reach the desired pitch. Modulation is introduced by rocking your finger back and forth (just as a violin player rocks his left hand on the neck of the violin) and trill is achieved by tapping the strip at a specific point. The note will then jump from its initial pitch to that corresponding to the position touched on the strip.

● The Joystick. This is an all-in-one mechanism.

LEVERS:▼
Oberheim are one of the few companies to employ up/down levers. Both are centre sprung, the left being for pitchbend, the right for modulation.

The stick can move left/right for pitchbend, and up/down for modulation (see p.83). The left/right movement is centre sprung so that the pitch remains constant when the lever is released. This mechanism, primarily utilised by Korg, is not too popular because it isn't particularly satisfying to use.

Portamento and Glissando

Portamento and Glissando are two further aspects of performance synthesis that have their controls conveniently located for real-time manipulation. Both these effects can be particularly impressive if used sensibly.

Consider firstly a monophonic instrument. If you play two notes the voice will jump from one pitch to the next. However, by introducing portamento and playing the new note instead of an instantaneous jump, the pitch of the note slides up or down from the first note to the new one (see figure 96). The speed at which

PORTAMENTO AND GLISSANDO

it does this is known as the Portamento rate, and a control for setting this rate is often to be found on the performance control panel. Effectively, when there is no portamento, the rate is very very fast, giving the impression of the jump between notes being instantaneous.

Glissando is a very similar effect but instead of the pitch smoothly sweeping between notes, glissando causes the pitch to step in semi-tones between the pitches.

We can draw an acoustic analogy for these two effects. If we bow an open violin string and then move a finger up the string, the pitch will rise smoothly. However, if we play a low note on a flute, the only way to slide up to a new pitch is to move in semi-tone steps – glissando.

The use of these effects is easily controlled when using a monophonic synthesizer, but things become more confusing when working with polyphony. The same basic effect is taking place, with the notes sliding from one pitch to another. The problem occurs in knowing what pitch is going to move to where. Imagine you have a four voice polyphonic synthesizer. Play a four note C major chord (C-E-G-C), then release that chord and play the top and bottom notes of the keyboard (say). You will find that the pitch will slew up to the top note and down to the bottom one. But where from? the portamento/glissando system works by sliding from the last note assigned to that voice – the top and the bottom note played could have been assigned to any one of the four previously played notes. Therefore, although the rate of travel is fixed (by the portamento control), there is no way of telling when each note is going to reach its new destination as you cannot know how 'far' the note has to travel.

Thus, although polyphonic portamento/glissando sounds very impressive with notes swirling all over the place, musically it is virtually impossible to control effectively.

Other Types of Controller

The keyboard need not be the only kind of controller. It just so happens that it is the most efficient, though not necessarily the most expressive.

There are two separate paths to the use of various controllers: i) the controller can either interface directly, via a specifically dedicated connection, to the central processor and voice production circuitry of the main body of the instrument; or ii) thanks to the advent of MIDI (see p. 103), the heart of a MIDI based instrument can be controlled by any device that outputs a MIDI code.

Naturally, the various alternative synthesizer controllers are based on existing acoustic instruments. Therefore a wind player (say) doesn't have to completely learn new skills and techniques; he can adapt his existing expertise.

The Guitar Synthesizer

Over the past few years, there have been three distinct types of guitar synthesizer. First the guitar control was developed. This sensed which strings and frets were being played and put out a monophonic control voltage and trigger pulse accordingly, to the standard synthesizer voice module. This wasn't a very satisfactory arrangement, as basically it was only a switching device – it didn't utilize any of the control qualities that a guitar can offer, in particular the bending of strings to raise the pitch. The monophonic guitar synthesizer was the next to appear, again providing a single control voltage and trigger output, but deriving this signal from the actual pitch produced by the guitar. The problems associated with this configuration centre around the ability of the pitch-to-voltage converter to track the notes being played. The guitarist must therefore play very clearly and precisely, making sure that only one note at a time sounds. The control voltage is fed to a standard voice module as before.

The most popular type of guitar synthesizer seems to be the polyphonic, or, more accurately, hexaphonic, models. Here, each string of the guitar generates its own control voltage and gate/trigger pulse. This information is sent down a multi-core cable often to a floor-mounted control unit where all the circuitry is housed. In order to keep costs down, the voltage controlled filter is sometimes shared by the six signal generators. The guitar synthesizer has never been as popular as many manufacturers first expected, and consequently, comparatively little has been done to promote this type of instrument as the logical replacement for the electric guitar.

The Wind Synthesizer

Strange as the concept might seem, the use of a wind-like instrument as a monophonic controller does make a lot of sense. The actual fingering of a wind instrument is easily translated to a control voltage, determining the pitch. However, it is with the wind sensor, (the part that is "blown"), that all the interesting things take place. All the shaping, expression and intonation of the sound produced by a wind instrument come from the mouthpiece, so the wind sensor automatically becomes the amplitude contour generator – the harder one blows, the greater voltage sent to the VCA – there's no ADSR envelope generator. The synthesizer voice module used is otherwise fairly standard.

A derivative of the wind synthesizer is the breath controller – the same sensor that is used in the mouthpiece. This device is used in conjunction with keyboard based synths as an extra performance control. The sensor detects how hard you are blowing a note and induces a control signal accordingly. This signal can then be used for amplitude and timbral manipulation.

Percussion Synthesizers/Electronic Drum Kits

This area has seen a massive growth over recent years – primarily due to the UK based firm of Simmons Electronics. An electronic drum consists of a pad with a sensor, possibly an inexpensive contact microphone, built into it. When hit, a control signal is induced in proportion to the applied force and the position on the head of the drum struck. This signal will then activate the voice circuitry of the associated module.

Percussion synthesizer controllers (the pads), by their very nature, are not generally used as a source of pitch information. They simply provide timing and force data, i.e. the signal derived from the pad consists of a trigger pulse stating when the note was hit, and a control signal proportional to the force with which the pad was struck. The trigger pulse is used to 'fire' the envelope generator, and the force information can be routed to vary the amplitude and/or the timbre of the percussion voice.

There are two main kinds of percussion synthesizer/electronic drum kit voice.

● based on the subtractive synthesizer, with oscillators and noise generators providing the basic pitch, filters with EGs (envelope generators) determining the timbre, and the VCA/EG combination setting the amplitude. As these are percussive voicings, the EGs have no sustain phase.

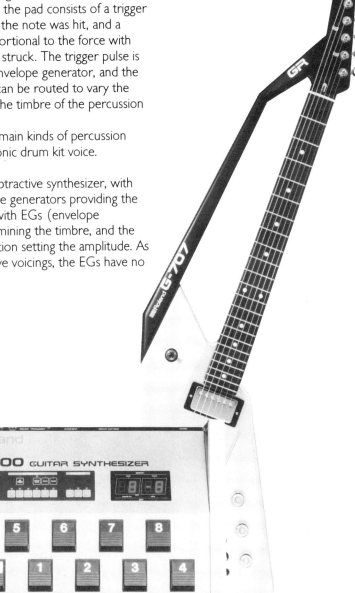

● Sampled Sounds. Every time a sound is triggered a digitally sampled recording of a particular drum voice is activated. The force information can be used to determine the amplitude and, in some instances, timbre of the sound.

For more information on percussion synthesizers, electronic drum kits etc., please consult "The Electronic Percussion Handbook", also published by Music Sales.

The Control Panel

Over the past few years the control panels of synthesizers have evolved considerably. In the past, it was natural enough to expect every parameter to have its own control knob or switch, but with the advent of digital control techniques the system known as "control assignment" has evolved.

Hardware and assembly costs play a crucial role in the final pricing of an electronic musical product, so ways in which the amount of hardware or assembly time can be reduced are of prime concern to manufacturers. Control assignment is an obvious way to make savings in both these areas, and thus make the instrument far more attractively priced.

With this system there is just one master control to which is assigned the parameter you wish to vary. The assignment is done either by pressing a switch that corresponds to that parameter (which in fact doesn't result in that great a saving as you still require a separate switch for each parameter); or by giving each parameter a control code. This requires just ten switches in the form of a simple key-pad, so to assign the filter cut-off frequency to the master control, you might punch-in code '41', say.

There is some resistance to this type of control system. It is far slower to use than having a separate control for each parameter, and it is much harder to shape sounds to your own requirements, but the financial savings are considerable, and the instrument usually looks more attractive in appearance.

The Programmer

If you are using a programmable synthesizer your instrument will feature a bank of switches for selecting the programmed sounds. Generally this will be in the form of a keypad (ten buttons numbered 0-9) and if the instrument is of the "control assignment" variety (see above) the same keypad that is used to select the parameters is probably also used to select programs.

With a conventional control panel the creation of your own programs is simple. You simply twiddle all the knobs and flick all the

switches until you are producing the sound you desire. These settings are then recorded digitally in one of the instrument's memory banks. You can then continue to twiddle all the knobs until you're happy with the next sound, then record it in a different memory location.

With a control assignment instrument the programming generally requires you to start with one of the programmed sounds then successively edit it (select a parameter, change it as necessary, select another parameter, adjust that to suit, etc. etc). This is a lengthy and rather unsatisfactory approach; you will often find that you are distracted and end up producing a completely different sound from that originally intended.

Certain instruments (such as the Yamaha DX-7) offer a Voice Initialise facility to help in the programming of new sounds. This sets up the instrument in its most basic format, and you gradually and methodically, work your way through the various parameters until you derive your 'ultimate' sound. This can then be written in the instrument's memory bank.

A synthesizer's programmer has only a limited memory capacity, and can therefore store only so many voicings. Manufacturers offer several options to extend the voicing storage potential of an instrument.

● Tape Dump. This enables the digital information that constitutes the sound (i.e. the settings of all the controls) to be fed on to a simple audio cassette recorder. Remember, it is digital information that is being recorded (bleeps and blurps) not the actual sound of that note. Once the contents of the programmer have been 'dumped', the instrument's memory is freed, and so another set of your own sounds can be programmed. These in turn are then 'dumped', or 'downloaded' on to tape. When you want to recall one of these sounds you simply play back the relevant piece of tape into the synthesizer, the data on the tape goes back into the instrument's memory, and you can recall your previously programmed sound.

● Plug-in Memory Expansion. This generally takes the form of a RAM (Random Access Memory) pack (see p.93), which contains a set of memory chips. The sounds you are programming can then be fed into this memory pack rather than into the instrument's own memory. The RAM pack will store this data even when removed from the instrument. Thus many sets of sounds can be collected - one set for each RAM pack then when you want a specific sound back, you simply plug in the appropriate RAM and call up the sound from the external rather than the internal memory location.

INTERFACING & ACCESSORIES

This chapter deals with the many devices that can be used to enhance the power and performance of the synthesizer. The beauty of today's synthesizers is that they need not become obsolescent with the advance of technology. A home organ or an electronic piano is a dedicated piece of equipment with the sole job of creating a specific sound, and there's little scope for add-ons. A synthesizer however, especially one equipped with the new MIDI interface, can be expanded with new pieces of equipment as and when they become available.

Before looking at the various items of hardware available, it is necessary to examine the various ways in which electronic musical instruments talk to one another.

Practical Interfacing

When considering the linking together of various instruments, the most important data to be transmitted is note information – i.e. what notes are played and when. There are three main ways in which this is done:

1 CV and Gate data. This convention was found on most synthesizers that appeared in the 70s and early 80s. Every time a note was played a trigger pulse (used to 'fire' the envelope generators) and a control voltage corresponding to the note being played (sent to the VCOs), would be generated. Sockets on the rear panel enabled these control signals to be fed to an external device, and similarly CV and Gate Inputs facilitated the control of the instrument's voice circuitry from an external source. Naturally, if the instrument were 8-voice polyphonic, 8 sets of CV and Gate Outs would be required as well as 8 sets of CV and Gate Ins. So although this system was manageable for monophonics, the 32 sockets required for the above 8-voice instrument became a little impractical.

Another problem with the CV and Gate system was that manufacturers developed all manner of different types of control signal. For example, some would use the one volt per octave CV convention, while others would use the 1000Hz per volt system, but the two were not compatible. Similarly, different trigger pulses would be used. Consequently you could usually interface only products made by the same company.

2 Digital Communication Bus (DCB). This system was developed and used primarily by the Roland Corporation. With more and more machines using microprocessors and being digitally controlled, Roland decided that the CV and Gate system was unsuitable for dealing with polyphonic instruments. So they developed a single interface that transmitted all the note information digitally. It was an extremely good idea but the main problem was that only Roland products were fitted with the DCB interface; it was incompatible with products made by any other manufacturer. Consequently a new interface was sought.

3 Musical Instrument Digital Interface (MIDI). The major synthesizer manufacturers got together and decided that it was in everyone's best interest to have a universal interface which enabled instruments and accessories to 'talk' with one another. The MIDI interface utilises a single 5-pin DIN connector, and this can handle up to 16 polyphonic voices simultaneously. In addition to note information, MIDI can also carry many other useful data, such as pitchbending, key velocity, program format data, sync pulses, etc. For a more detailed account of MIDI and the facilities it offers see p.103.

Having established that it is desirable to have instruments and accessories talking to one another, we should now look at the implementation of interfacing and at the devices available.

Coupling

The simplest example of interfacing must be 'coupling'. If we have two synthesizers linked together (let's say by means of a MIDI connector – figure 97) then by playing on one keyboard we will automatically trigger the other. For example, if the chord of Cmaj (C,E,G) were played on synth A, then Synth B would play those same notes although no-one was touching the keyboard. So, we can 'layer'

(see p. 103) voices from two different synthesizers on top of one another, which can vastly expand the creative power. This is of particular use if employing two completely different types of instrument (say an FM synthesizer with a subtractive variety), whence we could marry the two sounds to give a completely new range of timbres.

In the example illustrated there is just one MIDI connection shown with data transmitted from Synth A to Synth B. Here 'A' is known as the master, and 'B' the slave.

CONNECTIONS

SYNTHESIZER A

CONTROL LINK

OUTPUT

SYNTHESIZER B

OUTPUT

97

Synthesizer Voice Modules

The above set-up can be seen to make one of the keyboard controllers redundant so several manufacturers have been introducing polyphonic voice modules. These can either take the form of complete synthesizers with control panels but minus the keyboard controller (e.g. KORG's EX-800), or of polyphonic voice modules that primarily receive program data from the master instrument via MIDI (Yamaha's TX-816).

Again this can be taken a step further with the advent of the remote controller. This is a keyboard such as the KX-88 from Yamaha that has no voice circuitry whatsoever in it. It is used to drive and control one or more synthesizer voice modules, which are located away from the player – usually in a racking system.

KORG EX 800

KORG SQD-1

YAMAHA QX1

The Sequencer

The Sequencer is probably the most useful of all synthesizer accessories. Since MIDI revolutionised the whole synthesizer add-on industry the power of the sequencer has grown and grown until now you can do more with a good sequencer than you can with a multi-track tape recorder (though of course you cannot record acoustic sounds).

The sequencer is a form of controller. It has to be told exactly what to do, then it plays the synthesizer/voice modules for you, exactly as you've instructed it. The sequencer has many uses, but today it has come to the forefront as a compositional aid.

There are two main categories of Sequencer:

1) The Analogue Sequencer

The first generation of sequencers were of the analogue format. These devices still have their uses, albeit completely different from those of the far more common digital sequencer.

An analogue sequencer generates control voltages and trigger pulses, and it is therefore used only with other CV and Gate type synthesizers. The most common usage of the analogue sequencer is with modular synthesizers, when the device can be incredibly powerful; otherwise its use is primarily with monophonic synthesizers.

The workings of this control mechanism are quite simple. See figure 98. In this example there are three rows of 8 control knobs (channels A, B, and C). Each channel is used to control a certain parameter – say pitch, timbre, and amplitude. Each vertical set of three controls is selected sequentially by means of a master clock. So each step is set up to provide the desired effect, and each time a clock pulse occurs the master channel outputs adopt the control voltages of the next set of knobs. So we have a simple 8-step sequence of notes, each of equal duration, which cycles round and round until the master clock is stopped.

The analogue sequencer was used to great effect on the electronic disco records of the late 70's, particularly for simple repetitive bass riffs. As can be seen, however, its powers are limited. The above figure shows an 8-step sequencer for reasons of clarity, but most devices offered at least 12 or 16 steps.

Figure 98 shows a typical application of an analogue sequencer. Note that the clock of this device is voltage controlled, and that the output from Channel C is being fed back into the CV for the clock. This enables the Channel C controls to be used to set the duration of each note, thus enabling the sequencer to get away from producing the rather monotonous equal step sequences. In this example Channel A is being fed to one oscillator, and Channel B to another, so 2-note chords can be programmed. This facility is dependent on the CV inputs of the sequencer which is driven.

It may seem an obvious point to make, but many people fail to realise that if the sequencer is being used with a monophonic synthesizer you will not be able to play along with the sequence. The sequencer will be using the instrument's voice module, and thus all you can do by playing the instrument's keyboard is transpose the sequence.

2) Digital Sequencers

The analogue sequencer, like a controller such as the keyboard, is a one-way device. It sends data to the synthesizer; there's no input of data, other than that set up on its control panel. A digital sequencer, however, is a form of controller data storage device. It receives controller data from the keyboard (or from whatever device it is being used with), stores it, then regenerates that information and sends it on to the main body of the synthesizer on demand.

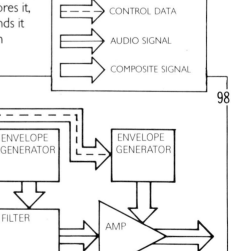

KEY
----> CONTROL DATA
--> AUDIO SIGNAL
--> COMPOSITE SIGNAL

THREE CHANNEL EIGHT STEP SEQUENCER

98

CLOCK RATE

START STOP   STEP

TRIGGER/GATE PULSE

CLOCK VOLTAGE INPUT

A   B   C

OSCILLATOR ONE

OSCILLATOR TWO

ENVELOPE GENERATOR

ENVELOPE GENERATOR

FILTER

AMP

OUTPUT

The sequencer is generally set into Record mode (just like a tape recorder) and a passage is played on the keyboard controller. The digital data representing these notes are then sent to the sequencer and stored. Upon Playback this information is simply passed on to the synthesizer and turned into sound.

Most of today's digital sequencers are polyphonic, i.e. they will record several notes at once. There are several kinds of these devices, but most fall into either the Step Time or Real Time categories.

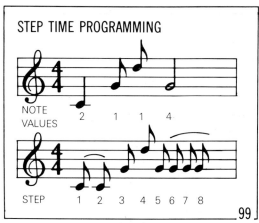

STEP TIME PROGRAMMING

NOTE VALUES 2 1 1 4

STEP 1 2 3 4 5 6 7 8

99

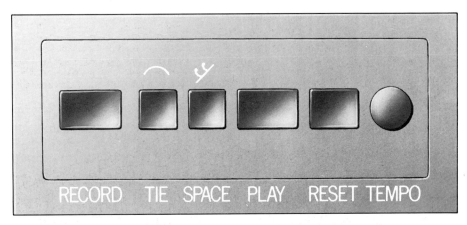

RECORD   TIE   SPACE   PLAY   RESET   TEMPO

Step Time Sequencers

As the name implies, a step time sequencer produces a sequence made up of a string of steps of equal length. The advantage of this is that very little memory is taken up by the sequence. Therefore you will often find this type of sequencer built into a polyphonic synthesizer.

A typical set of step time sequencer controls can be seen in the figure. The device is set into Record mode and a chord is played on the keyboard. These notes will then be assigned to the first step of the sequence; the next step is automatically selected and whatever notes are then played are registered for that step, and so on. At the end of the sequence the Play button can be pressed, and back will come the programmed notes – but all will be of the same length (rather like the original analogue sequence).

To introduce an element of timing it is necessary to use the 'Tie' and 'Space' buttons. So if we wanted to sequence the bar of music shown in Figure 99, which features quavers, crotchets, and a minim, we would decide to make one step equivalent to a quaver (the shortest note). A crotchet would therefore require 2 tied steps, and a minim 4 tied steps. So the bar would last 8 steps and be programmed as shown. This is just one bar. Most step time sequencers offer a step capacity of the order of 500-1000 steps; therefore you could have a sequence of up to 100 bars length

if you didn't require notes or rests shorter than a quaver. Or if a greater resolution (shorter notes) is required then proportionally less bars will be available.

Real Time Sequencers

A Real Time sequencer bears a very close comparison with an actual tape recorder, only this time controller information in the form of digital codes is being stored. The sequencer is put into Record mode and all note information is derived from the keyboard/controller. All the timing information will be stored along with the pitch data, so upon Playback the recorded sequence is faithfully recalled. To anyone with his eyes closed it would be as if the notes were being played live there and then.

Real time digital sequencers can be incredibly sophisticated, especially since the MIDI connection (see p.103) enables such a wide variety of data to be transmitted, and hence stored. Not only will some of today's sequencers store note data, but also velocity and pressure control signals, pitchbend, and even program changes. But the most impressive and important feature of real time sequencers that utilise MIDI is the "multi-tracking" facility.

MIDI enables you to assign every note recorded to one of 16 MIDI channels, so upon playback any synthesizer connected to the sequencer will play those notes that are assigned to the selected MIDI channel One line of music could be recorded in order to play back on MIDI Ch.I, then a second line could be superimposed on that sequence, but assigned to Ch 2. and so on. On replay, the two synthesizers in the system receive the correct information, and can thus render the piece with the correct voicings.

This facility can be expanded up to 16 tracks, assuming that you have enough synthesizers or synthesizer voice modules to provide the sounds. So in essence a multi-track facility can be realised without even having a tape recorder. More on this subject can be found in the section dealing with MIDI.

Spatial Effects

Electronic musical instruments generally produce what is known as a "dry" signal. That is to say the sound is not very vibrant or lively. This is because the instrument is producing purely electronic signals and the environment hasn't had a chance to react with the sound. When you listen to a church organ, for example, you are hearing not only the pipes, but also the effect the church building has on the sound. It's as if the church is actually part of the instrument. If you were to take the organ and set it up in a room with no ambience, the character of the instrument would be totally different. It is partly for this reason that the signals produced by the synthesizer are usually processed further by external devices in order to enhance their sound and to provide some extra presence.

These devices are usually termed spatial effects generators as they can be used to give the illusion that you are hearing the sound in a wide range of different environments.

Echo and Reverberation

The most important spatial effects unit that you can purchase for a synthesizer is a reverberation unit. To understand what reverberation is, it is first necessary to consider the subject of echo.

We all know what an echo is. We're standing on the proverbial side of a mountain, and shout out a witty phrase or saying and the sound bounces off the mountain opposite and comes back to us a second or two later. So echo is a simple and distinct repeat of a sound a period of time after the original. There are two relevant 'echo' measurements. The repeat rate (or delay time), which is the time between the original sound and the echo; and the echo intensity, i.e. how loud the echo is in comparison with the original. Obviously in the case of a naturally occurring echo the amplitude of the echo would be smaller than the original, though when using an electronic simulation this need not be so.

The echo repeat time could be virtually any period . . . one second . . . ten seconds etc. But in fact it can't be less than around one tenth of a second. Why? Because the human ear cannot distinguish sounds that occur within a tenth of a second of one another; the two merge to form a single sound. Reverberation is made up of a series of echoes with different repeat times and intensities. The echoes' times are all very close to one another – within a tenth of a second, so they merge into a composite sound and no individual echoes can, therefore, be perceived by the human ear.

Figure 100 explains this acoustic phenomenon. The sound emanates from point A, and is heard by the listener at point B. Some sound travels directly to the listener, and is heard virtually instantaneously. But a lot of sound is reflected from the walls, floor and ceiling of the room before reaching the listener, and therefore the sound takes longer to arrive. There are countless numbers of reflected vibrations which merge to form a single reverberative sound.

There are four main ways in which reverberation can be simulated.

I The reverb spring: the audio signal is fed to a transducer (a device that runs the electrical sound into physical movement) which is connected to a taut spring. The signal causes the spring to vibrate, and these vibrations are picked up by a second transducer at the other end of the spring, which turns the original signal

REVERBERATION:
Any partially enclosed environment will have some form of reverberative effect on a sound. Here the sound emanating from the loudspeaker can take many different paths to the listener. Each reflection takes a different amount of time to reach the listener, and will arrive at different intensities. Consequently a 'lively' reverberative sound ensues. The digital reverberation unit (illustrated – LEXICON PCM-60) is capable of recreating this addition of delays. Large ambient halls or small echoey rooms can be created by utilising different algorithms.

THE LEXICON PCM 60
DIGITAL REVERB CHAMBER

NATURAL REVERBERATION

100

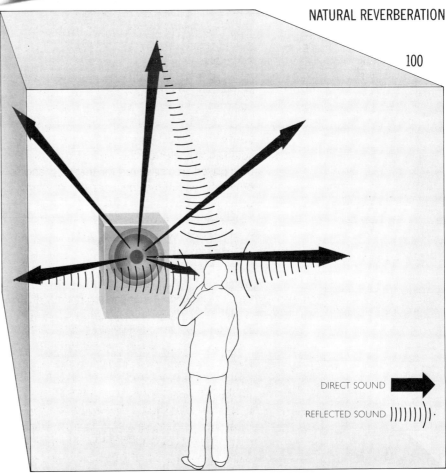

DIRECT SOUND

REFLECTED SOUND

plus a lot of extra vibrations back into an electrical signal. The signal, as it reaches the end of the spring, is reflected back up the spring so you get a series of sound reflections that simulate the reverberative effect. The main problem with a spring reverb unit is its very poor high frequency response; consequently it is prone to sound 'twangy' when used with percussive sounds.

2 The reverb plate: this works on a similar principle to the spring reverb, except that a large sheet of metal is used in place of the spring. This gives a better high frequency response, and a more realistic effect, but this is unfortunately reflected in the cost.

3 The echo chamber: here a room is actually used to create the effect. The sound is fed into the room via a loudspeaker, and a microphone is positioned so as to pick up the enriched sound. The result is controlled by the position of the microphone with respect to the speaker. The problem with this system is that it is usually somewhat impracticable, and the chamber has to be free of any extraneous noises.

4 The digital reverb: this device has become extremely popular over recent years. The source sound is turned into a digital number, then fed down a delay line. At various points down the line, the signal is picked off and fed back to the input. Each feedback loop represents a reflection. So the digital delay can be amazingly accurate in the type of reverb effect obtained. It is conveniently housed in a small (usually rack-mounted) case.

Unfortunately these are also rather expensive devices.

Reverberation is a useful tool for the synthesist, especially when you are involved in simulating acoustic instruments, as these will rarely be heard 'dry'. Undoubtedly it should be the first signal processor acquisition.

The Delay Line

A digital delay line (DDL) is also an extremely powerful processing device. This is due primarily to its flexibility. With a DDL you can create multi-echo, phasing, flanging, slap-back echo, chorusing/automatic double tracking effects, and sampling – a useful array of effects.

Figure 101 illustrates the workings of a DDL. In essence the device takes the audio signal fed to it and outputs that same signal a short period later. Generally the delay times are between a few milliseconds and a handful of seconds. But to enable the device to be more useful you will notice one or two refinements.

FEEDBACK – this control takes a part of the output and routes it back to the input, so repeat echoes can be established. Were it not for this facility you would hear just a single repeat. Feedback enables a series of echoes to be derived from just the one sound.

MODULATION – the delay period is set by a master control. But it is possible to vary this time using a low frequency oscillator. The rate and depth of the variation can be set using the modulation section and this enables effects such as chorusing, flanging and phasing to be recreated. All these effects require a delay time of around 40 milliseconds, and flanging requires a degree of feedback to be introduced.

SAMPLING – this button enables you to fill up the delay line with a sound, then to recall it as and when necessary. So instead of feeding a sound into the delay which automatically comes out at the other end a period of time later, the sound is held within the delay line until a trigger signal is received (from a button, footswitch, or some external controller) when the stored sound is fed out. The sample's length is, naturally, limited to the maximum delay time. The pitch of the sample upon 'Playback' can be varied by changing the setting of the delay time. And if this time can be set by some form of controller, then it is possible to 'play' the sampled sound.

The digital delay line is an extremely useful all-in-one effects unit, and is relatively inexpensive when compared with the cost of a digital reverberation unit.

TIME SHIFTING USING DELAY LINE

SIGNAL

REPLICATED SIGNALS

101

COMPUTERS & MUSIC 10

The Computer

Computers have been the main cause of the recent quantum jump in musical instrument technology. Most electronic musical instruments utilise a microprocessor as the central brain. This device organises the data supplied to it from various parts of the instrument (the keyboard, control panel, etc.), and turns it into useful control data which is routed to the voice modules. We will not delve too deeply into the realms of computer music, but it is useful to know a little about the workings of the microprocessor.

Microprocessors are common to many devices – you'll as likely as not find the same microprocessor chip in an electronic typewriter, or a microwave oven, as in a musical instrument. The systems differ by the instructions contained within the ROM (Read Only Memory). These instructions, which are preprogrammed at the design stage of the instrument, determine how the data will be treated and manipulated when fed to the microprocessor. The RAM (Random Access Memory) can be used as a temporary memory so that the microprocessor can carry out a task, then hold the resulting data in store for a period of time while it carries out some other task. The stored data can be recalled when required.

The use of a microprocessor in the majority of musical instruments gives rise to the term "dedicated", i.e. it is set up to perform a single task (running the instrument). A non-dedicated computer system is one that requires the user to feed the processor a new program (instruction set) every time it is used. This is far less convenient, but it does mean that the computer can be used for other tasks, e.g. word processing, accounts management, games etc.

A Non-Dedicated Computer Music System
The tell-tale sign of a non-dedicated system is a QWERTY (typewriter) keyboard. If it features such a keyboard, it is probably non-dedicated, and in addition to its musical role can be used for a wide range of other tasks. It will, therefore, require some instructions as to how it will run; this is the role of software.

Several different media can be used to handle the software. The most common are cassette, cartridge and floppy disc. Data is fed into the device via one of these storage devices and held in the Random Access Memory. The processor now has a set of instructions and can manipulate the data accordingly. When the power is turned off, however, the program is lost, and therefore it has to be loaded in every time the instrument is used.

A most impressive non-dedicated music orientated computer is Yamaha's CX-5, which is an MSX computer. (MSX is a standard format of computer, primarily marketed by Japanese companies; the name referring to the language it uses – Extended Microsoft.) The CX-5 is a simple home computer that has an eight note voice module fitted. Software programs can be fed in via a cartridge port, and then voicing, sequencing and composing can be effected using the instrument's alpha-numeric keyboard in conjunction with a separate chromatic (musical) keyboard.

At the other end of the spectrum is the Fairlight CMI, which is an expensive quasi-non-dedicated music facility, based on an Australian business computer. An extensive range of musical software is available for this instrument, and extra hardware, in the form of voice modules, has been added to let the computer 'sing'. The beauty of having a non-dedicated system such as this is its flexibility. When a new musical requirement is raised, the manufacturers can write a new piece of software that will enable the computer to perform this task, and if necessary extra hardware can also be added. One such example is the synchronization of a soundtrack to film. With the Fairlight, whole compositions can be realised and stored in the computer's memory. A piece can then be processed so that it lasts exactly the right length of time to match the film sequence. It can then be synchronized exactly using markers and/or time codes on the film soundtrack.

Dedicated Devices
Most electronic musical instruments are dedicated devices.

The most powerful sequencers are usually dedicated devices. For example, the Yamaha QX-1 is one of the most versatile and useful sequencers around. It can store over 80,000 notes, and it does so by having an enormous memory. This memory takes the form

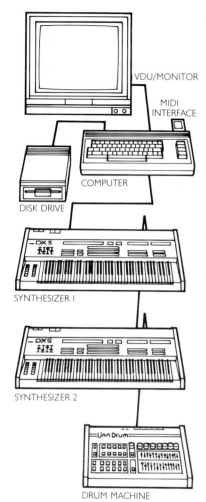

VDU/MONITOR

MIDI INTERFACE

COMPUTER

DISK DRIVE

SYNTHESIZER I

SYNTHESIZER 2

DRUM MACHINE

of a floppy disk. All the time it is recording or playing back sequences the processor is talking to the floppy disk where all the note data is stored. This breaks away from the more conventional RAM data storage system, but as a result the device can handle much more information at a far more economical cost.

Memories

READ ONLY MEMORIES (ROMs): These contain information that has been loaded during fabrication (akin to an LP record). The data cannot be changed. Used primarily to store program instructions, they can also take the form of separate plug-in cartridges, on which are stored preset voicing information (e.g. Yamaha's DX-7).

RANDOM ACCESS MEMORIES (RAMs): Data can be fed into these chips and changed at any point by the user, but the information will remain in the chips only as long as some power is being applied to the devices. When the power is turned off the data erases itself. This is used as a temporary "note-pad" memory for holding program instructions and data.

PROGRAMMABLE READ ONLY MEMORIES (PROMs): These are available as blank chips into which with the aid of a special machine, you can load your own data, or instruction set. Once you have fed in the information it is there permanently.

ERASABLE PROGRAMMABLE READ ONLY MEMORIES (EPROMs): Used primarily by manufacturers to store program data. If an update needs to be made in the control program, an EPROM can have its memory banks erased (normally by putting it under an ultraviolet light for 15-20 minutes), then reprogrammed with new instructions.

ELECTRONICALLY ERASABLE PROGRAMMABLE READ ONLY MEMORIES (EEPROMs): These devices equate to RAMs, only they do not need a back-up power supply to retain information. The RAM-1 cartridge available for the DX-7 contains EEPROM memory, but is an extremely expensive form of data storage. It is most convenient for holding voicing data however. In addition to these circuit based memory devices, various other media are used to store the large amounts of data that are required when dealing with voicing of instruments and sequences.

AUDIO CASSETTE: Many synthesizers

provide a tape dump facility which enables a simple audio cassette recorder to be connected. Data is then recorded in digital format on the tape, freeing the limited on-board memory for new sounds/sequences. When that data is next required the tape is replayed into the instrument/sequencer; the information is thus re-loaded. This is a very cheap form of data storage but slow and awkward to use, primarily because the tape has to be continually rewound to the right place.

FLOPPY DISC: A much faster but more expensive system. Here a small magnetic disc is used in conjunction with a disc drive unit. The read/write head of the floppy disc drive can move quickly to any point on the disc; therefore time is not lost in spooling back and forth looking for data. A floppy disc can handle up to 800kbytes of memory – a considerable amount. It is particularly useful for storing the data used to construct a sampled sound, where 30-50kbytes of memory are required for every second of sample.

QUICK DISCS: These are the latest in low-cost memory units, and are much smaller and more rugged than the floppy disc. They run sequentially like an audio cassette, which slows down the process somewhat, but their actual read/write mechanism is extremely fast.

The Synthesizer and the Computer

The computer has already taken over the internal control of electronic musical instruments, and this has led to remarkable advances in terms of value for money and reliability. When synthesizers first appeared, their biggest single problem was tuning. The pitch of the oscillators would drift all over the place. With digital and computer technology such problems are eliminated.

But the computer has also affected the electronic instrument industry in a different way. As well as dedicated instruments becoming better and less expensive, we are now seeing a growth in the use of the domestic home computer for musical purposes. Most home computers are equipped with some form of sound production facility, and an increasing amount of software is now coming on stream that enables the enthusiast to create new sounds, program sequences and even multi-layer tracks into complete compositions. And with the advent of MIDI (see p.103) it is now possible (by purchasing an interface box) to get a cheap home computer to control any MIDI equipped synthesizer. Music and Computing are finally joining hands.

USING THE SYNTHESIZER

11

Synthesis is an art, and as we shall see as we progress through this section, it can stand more than one analogy with a far more traditional artform – that of painting.

The preceding chapters should have made you reasonably familiar with the various "nuts and bolts" of the synthesizer. Now we can see how the synthesizer can most effectively be used. As there are so many different types of instrument, this section obviously has to be fairly broad based. However, you should glean some useful playing tips as well as perhaps understanding the concepts behind synthesis a little more clearly.

Roles

The use of the synthesizer can be grouped under four basic headings: Imitative, Impressionistic, Abstract (sometimes called Imaginative) and Effects ("FX") Synthesis. These headings have nothing to do with the instrument's hardware, but concern themselves with the way in which the synthesizer is used.

In order to capture the qualities of any sound, the synthesist has to know his instrument inside out. With the more conventional subtractive instruments this comes with practice, but many owners of instruments

utilising FM synthesis, and to some extent PD synthesis, experience difficulty in programming new sounds, and getting the desired effect is something of a hit and miss affair. Such owners can take heart from the fact that these synthesizers usually come equipped with a wide range of preset sounds, and a great deal can be done by adopting different playing styles to match the desired effect.

However, if you are fully cognizant with the working of your synthesizer you will have a great advantage, and with practice you will find you go instinctively to the correct parameters in order to produce the desired sound.

Obviously, the better the synthesizer the greater the scope for accurately creating sounds, but even the most basic of variable synthesizers will provide the opportunity to simulate most existing instruments, and to develop a wide range of unique new sounds and special effects.

Imitative Synthesis

The term "synthesizer" implies the artificial creation of something, and originally the electronic music synthesizer was thought of as a device used for copying the sounds of existing instruments – known as Imitative Synthesis. And in fact the synthesizer can be used to simulate pretty well any acoustic and electric instrument. This may seem a rather sweeping statement, but broadly speaking it is true, with one or two reservations.

The ability to recreate every instrument of the orchestra from one device has its attractions, though maybe not for the members of the orchestra. But of course the synthesizer cannot emulate every nuance of every instrument.

The good imitative synthesist not only has to be a good player, and to know his synthesizer, but also a good listener. Like the great portrait or landscape painters, they have to understand the medium with which they are working. They have to have artistic ability, but above all they have to be able to "see" what they are doing and how it relates to the overall picture. The

Trevor Horn first came into the public eye with Bruce Wolley on the classic "Video Killed The Radio Star". The duo then went on to replace Rick Wakeman in the awesome electroclassic band Yes. Horn is now best known as the producer of Frankie Goes To Hollywood and the man who made Fairlight a household word.

IMITATING SOLO VIOLIN

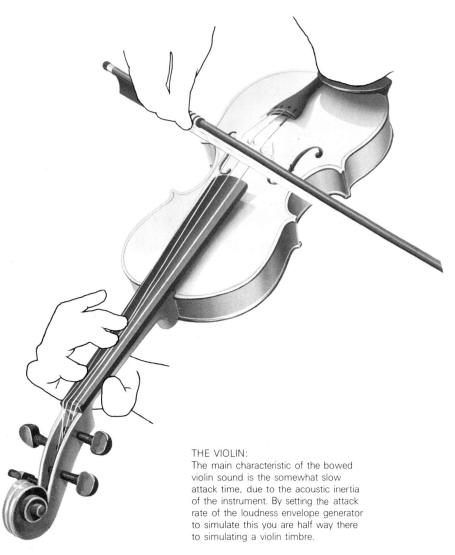

THE VIOLIN:
The main characteristic of the bowed violin sound is the somewhat slow attack time, due to the acoustic inertia of the instrument. By setting the attack rate of the loudness envelope generator to simulate this you are half way there to simulating a violin timbre.

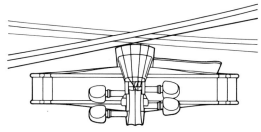

synthesist has to be able to hear the sound and understand its makeup.

When you are trying to simulate a particular instrument you don't usually have a point of reference, i.e. if you are simulating a violin sound, you unfortunately won't have a top violin player sitting beside you giving you a perfect example of what you are striving for. It is often worth putting on a record that features the instrument in question. Listen not only to its timbral make-up, but also how it is played.

Selecting Characteristics

The real secret of good imitative synthesis is to be able to pick out the characteristic nuances

of a sound, to recreate them, and to play the sound as it would be played by the original instrument. The rest is surprisingly unimportant.

Consider a solo violin passage played with a bow. What do we hear that tells us we are listening to a violin? Well, at this stage the pitch is unimportant (although of course it has to fall within the range of the violin); the tone of the note does play a fairly large part in the overall sound-picture; but in fact the two most important elements of a violin sound are the attack phase and the characteristic delayed vibrato. The attack phase of a bowed violin note isn't instantaneous, there's a build up to the note, an acoustic inertia. This has to be accounted for in setting up the sound. Also, if you listen to a violinist playing a sustained note, you will notice that he usually introduces vibrato to the note to animate it. This can easily be simulated by virtually all types of synthesizer using the low frequency oscillator. Of course you still have to ensure that the other parameters are in line with the violin sound, but if you can pick out the instrument's prime characteristics you are well on your way to a good imitation.

Let's take the clarinet as our second example. The giveaway here is definitely its timbre, which is in fact very closely allied in harmonic structure to a square wave. In addition the initial attack phase is quite fast, which is also important, and the release phase must generally be fast otherwise a completely different effect will result.

The clarinet is one of the simplest sounds to simulate; therefore, if you do have a synthesizer, try to create this sound from scratch. You shouldn't have any real problems. Even with FM synthesis it is a relatively simple proposition to create a square wave by modulating one operator (the carrier) at frequency 1.00, by a second operator (the modulator) of frequency 2.00. The modulator should be 2/3 of the maximum amplitude of the carrier or 0.66 on the Output Level readout if you are using a DX machine.

Interestingly, it is the attack phase that is by far the most important when imitating other sounds. The reason for this is because we are all basiclly lazy. When you read a book your eyes scan the page looking for something to recognise; if we see a group of letters whose pattern resembles that of a word whose meaning fits the sense of the sentence then our brains register the fact, and we move on to the next word without having studied each and every letter. Did you spot that 'basically' in the sentence before last was spelt incorrectly? Well, we do the same thing with sound. We hear the initial part of our sound and the brain registers the fact that what is being heard seems to be a violin. Only if the ensuing part of the sound is out of character does our brain react. If the sound seems pretty well right then the benefit of the doubt is given.

The main point to grasp at this stage is that even if you are using the most basic synthesizer you can still create a wide range of imitative effects. You just have to be cunning. Everything's on your side. Just analyse closely the sound you want to recreate and use your brain before you start twiddling knobs, as once you're at the instrument you will inevitably be sidetracked.

There are some obvious pitfalls to bridge before getting down to recreating a particular sound. The type of synthesizer you are using is one such factor. If it is a monophonic instrument you will have problems recreating polyphonic instruments such as piano, harpsichord etc. Okay, this may sound obvious, but it is necessary to realise this. In most cases you won't even be able to accurately simulate single notes that would be played on an instrument such as an acoustic piano. This is because when a note has been played, the sound lingers and if you move to a new note, the residual release phase of the first note will be abruptly cut off, thus destroying the sound's natural quality.

Conversely, if you are recreating a solo voice, such as a flute, on a polyphonic synthesizer, then you will find that the release phase of the previous note may continue when a new one is played. This again will destroy the realism, so the synthesizer should be put into mono, or solo mode.

Touch sensitivity is also a vital requirement if you want to produce an accurate piano simulation. Okay, so you can make a good piano sound with a non-sensing controller, but with all notes coming out with the same timbre/ amplitude, you will not be able to convince anyone that the sound you are making is that of the real thing. This area is dealt with more fully in the "Playing Style" section.

Impressionistic Synthesis

This category is closely allied to Imitative Synthesis, but instead of trying to accurately recreate the sound of a particular instrument, you are striving to produce a sound that does the same job – but doesn't necessarily have the exact characteristics of the original. A classic example of this is the string accompaniment. Ever since The Moody Blues had their "Nights in White Satin" hit, players have realised you don't have to have the real thing. On this track the strings were produced by a Mellotron (a 'Replay', or primitive sampling instrument,

CLARINET STYLE

CLARINET:
The characteristic timbre of the clarinet is very close to that of the square wave – as can be seen from the harmonic spectrum diagram. The appearance of certain even harmonics gives an extra fullness to the sound.

and although they have a string like quality, you would have difficulty convincing all but the most inebriated of musicians that there wasn't something seriously wrong with the 'orchestra' on that session. But the record worked because an impression of strings was given.

It was this demand for an instrument that could produce a string ensemble effect that led to so much development in polyphonic electronic keyboards in the 60s and 70s. String machines were yesterday's polyphonic synthesizers.

So, it isn't always necessary to be imitative. When using a synthesizer you have to consider what you want the sound to do. Is an up-front lead line sound required? – maybe use a flute like sound. Do you want a lush sustained chordal accompaniment? – use a string-like effect. Do you want rhythmic chordal punctuation? – try a stabbing brass sound. But realise that you don't have to get a perfect imitation of a four-piece brass section to communicate the flavour of the music.

Impressionistic and Imitative synthesis go hand in glove, especially when it comes to multi-track recording. A perfect copy of a trombone may sound great on its own, but, when blended into a complete arrangement, does not sound right. Similarly, an impressionistic guitar type sound may seem just like the real thing when "sat" in the mix, but when you hear it on its own it sounds completely different. The art of using synthesizers is a complex one, and only

THOMAS DOLBY:
One of the world's best known exponents of the electronic music synthesizer. Dolby's first ever synthesizer was a humble monophonic — a Micromoog. Today his arsenal of keyboards includes one of the most prestigious computer based music systems — the Fairlight CMI. Dolby was also one of the first musicians to use computers to control synthesizers — his early experimentations involved the use of a Commodore PET computer to drive an array of different instruments.

experience can teach you what works and what doesn't. There are few rules.

Playing Style

You could spend money on the best equipment until you are blue in the face, but you still won't get (say) a good string sound, or even a good impression of one unless you play the instrument in the correct manner.

Let's look more closely at the string example because it is indicative of most areas of impressionistic and imitative synthesis. The simple fact is that 61 notes on a keyboard do not equate to 16 pairs of hands – 8 holding a bow and 8 pressing strings on to a smooth piece of wooden board. So you have to think "string ensemble". You have to understand the string arranger's craft in order to be able to produce a convincing rendition of a piece of music played by a string section.

The best way is to get an arrangement (yes, the dots) out of the library and to see how that particular piece is constructed. If you are setting

out with your own original piece, you really do have to think things out. For example, block chords are out. String sections don't play them. Think of the piece in terms of Bass, Cello, Violas and Violins (perhaps leaving out the Bass if your technique is a little dodgy). Each of these instruments covers a certain area of the keyboard, so pull the chords apart so that they all get a "look in". Experience will tell you how much you can get away with, and to gain experience you have to listen a lot; listening to other pieces tells you what works and why.

The same advice should be heeded when working in the impressionistic field. If you want to create the feel of a string section using a somewhat differently voiced sound, then you still have to play in the style of the subject you are striving to suggest. Again, if you play block chords the synthesizer is going to sound like an organ.

The same process applies if you are imitating any type of instrument. Holding down an eight note chord isn't the best way to treat a timpani-drum simulation; introducing vibrato to an acoustic piano sound will instantly give the game away.

Like all good rules, the above rules are made to be broken. It's fun to play musical tricks using a synthesizer. For example, you can derive the ultimate guitar sound, and introduce a little pitch bend at the appropriate places in a solo, but then as the solo progresses the amount of bend can become greater and greater. This will grab your listener's attention until the next sound he expects is that of the strings breaking or the neck snapping. Similarly, sampling machines can be fun, especially if you are using the human voice. You can introduce all manner of effects, loops and pitchbends using the power of "out-of-contextness" to extremes.

The following examples illustrate the way in which various voicings can be created.

Solo Violin (bowed):

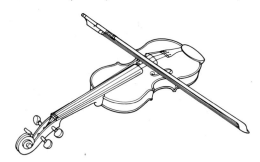

VOICING – As described above, with a slowish attack and delayed vibrato. Often a modulated pulse width waveform works well. No beating effect should be used. Little or no timbral change should occur during the note. The loudness contour should be sustained at a maximum value with a fairly fast release time.

PLAYING – The solo violin should be played smoothly over a fairly narrow range of notes. Portamento doesn't work very well, but the pitchbender can be used slowly to move between notes, but only if you have a good technique. An expression pedal can be a useful extra to control the overall volume.

Viola/Cello:

As above, but pitched in a lower register. The cello has a greater acoustic inertia than the violin so it may be necessary to increase the attack time slightly.

String Ensembles (Mantovani style):

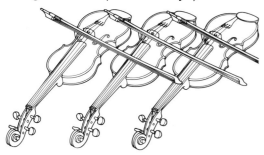

VOICING – The quality of spatial movement associated with this sound can be achieved by beating oscillators, by introducing pulse width modulation, or by feeding the output through a chorus unit or digital delay line. The timbre should remain fairly constant, and the amplitude envelope is much as for the solo strings, although the attack time can be still further prolonged. LFO modulation should be applied only if the effect is polyphonic (i.e. each voice has its own independent LFO).

PLAYING – Chords should be pulled well apart, i.e. stretched over as much of the keyboard as possible. No pitchbend or portamento should be introduced.

Brass:

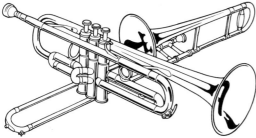

VOICING – Brass sounds are typified by a moving harmonic content, the sound brightening during the attack phase then the higher harmonics being removed during the release phase. A degree of instaneous modulation at the start of the note can be used to simulate the over-blowing sound. Generally, sawtooth waves are used for brass sounds. If possible, the sound can be enhanced for some

roles by setting two VCOs, or carrier oscillators, a fifth apart, thus greatly enriching the harmonic content of the sound. This approach may not work for certain polyphonic pieces as severe dissonance between pitches can be set up.

PLAYING – Polyphonic brass voicings should be played with only one hand, and then only over part of the span of the keyboard. This is because most synthesizers aren't really capable of simultaneously producing both low frequency and high frequency brass-like timbres. What's more, the sound becomes very muddy if a wide range of notes are all played at once.

Flutes:

Flutes generate very pure tones which can quite effectively be recreated using just an undoctored sine or triangle wave. If a more breathy and overblown flute sound is required, then you need to introduce some filtered white noise to 'dirty' the attack phase of the sound. Heavy ring modulation by the LFO running just

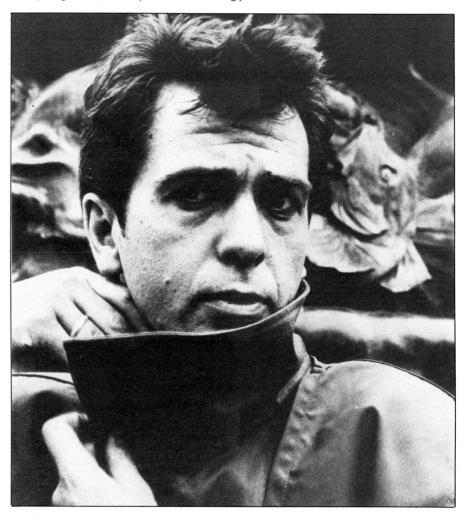

Peter Gabriel became known as the captivating visual focus for Genesis' highly theatrical stage performances. As a solo artist he has been not only a pioneer of new technology in music but also a forceful catalyst for the fusion of native South American and African music with Western synthesis.

in to the audio spectrum can be used to create the overblown effect, but this is difficult to get exactly right.

PLAYING – Flutes are generally heard either as solo instruments or in just two parts, so chordal flute arrangements are out, unless you want to produce a sound like a steam calliope (or fairground organ). Trills and a spritely playing style work well to give the flute a natural air.

Clarinet:
Similar principles as detailed for the flute apply, only use a square wave instead of a sine/triangle one.

Human Voice/Whistle:
One of the interesting characteristics of the human voice is that it often seems to start just below the pitch of the note and move quickly up into pitch. This may not be the case generally, but by gliding up into pitch, from half a semi-tone down, the loudness envelope reaches the end of its attack phase and seems to give a good impression of the human voice. The main body of the sound is generally best

ISAO TOMITA:
Along with Wendy Carlos, Tomita has been one of the pioneers of the use of the modular synthesizer. One of his characteristic devices is the use of a whistling timbre that takes up the melody line on occasions.

achieved by heavily filtering an LFO modulated pulse waveform. The effect also works well when simulating the human whistle, when a relatively high frequency sine wave should be used instead of the filtered PWM waveform, and also some delayed LFO frequency modulation should be applied. A fair splashing of reverberation works wonders on this voicing.
PLAYING – Long sustained notes are the most effective for a choir-like sound, with not too close chordal structures. The whistling effect is a solo one and should therefore be played monophonically – portamento can be used.

Electric and Electronic Organs:
VOICING – The classic 'electric' Hammond sound has two distinct characteristics – Its key click, and the rotary speaker effect. It is best recreated using a subtractive synthesizer with two beating oscillators' waveforms which are used to simulate the movement of the rotary speaker. The filter resonance needs to be turned up so that the filter almost oscillates, and with a very fast filter envelope spike, which produces the key click effect. The effect can be superb if the filter is correctly biased. The electronic organ, as typified by the Farfisas and Vox Continentals of the 60s, has a very thin sound, with a tell-tale constant vibrato. This is easy to recreate using pulse waves. No beating should be employed nor is there any timbral movement. The envelope is a straight gate On/Off.

PLAYING – There are no rules for playing a synthesizer when trying to recreate an organ sound. Most bands of the Sixties tended to play block chords on their electronic organs so that's acceptable, while playing full chords in particular sevenths gives the electric organ sound considerable punch. Neither of these instruments offers suitable opportunities for single note lead lines.

These are just some of the imitative and impressionistic possibilities open to the synthesist. There are many more. In fact you should be able to make a recognisable imitation of virtually any other musical instrument – though the saxophone is particularly difficult.

Abstract/Imaginative Synthesis

Few players use the synthesizer simply to copy other musical instruments. There is a whole new world of sounds just waiting to be 'realized'. Abstract, or imaginative, synthesis creates these unique musical timbres.

Abstract synthesis relies on the imagination and the musical awareness of the user. "Context" is the key word. To exploit this field you don't really have to be a technical wizard, but what you do need is the ability to recognise what sound works. A twinkling fairyland sound isn't well suited to a powerhouse heavy metal environment. That's an obvious example, but creating your own unique sounds is just half the battle; when you've got them, you have to use them correctly.

During the 'reign' of the analogue synthesizer in the late 70s and early 80s, you would hear similar sounds on all manner of different records. Players with Prophet 5s (or whatever) would mess around modifying the presets, then lock on to just a handful of different sounds. It is very easy to reach the situation where you have 'a sound for every occasion' then don't really bother creating new ones. The digital, sampling, and FM instruments of the present have led to many players rethinking their sounds, and consequently we are hearing a wider range of abstract synthesizer sounds then ever before.

With the appearance of cheaper sampling instruments such as the Mirage from Ensoniq, and AKAI's rack mounted MIDI controlled polyphonic sampler, we should soon start to hear some interesting developments in both popular and 'classical' electronic music.

When you are using a synthesizer for abstract work, don't get caught up in the normal programming track. Experiment and try new approaches to the sound. For example, with a dual VCO per voice analogue synthesizer use the oscillators at strange intervals apart; modulate the filter at very high frequencies; use inverted filtering; try feeding external sound sources into the filter (if possible). Tweaking various controls (that aren't performance controls), such as filter resonance, or amplitude attack time, while you are playing the instrument can lead to some extremely interesting sounds. This will give you another medium for injecting expression; that is if you have the spare hand.

With FM synthesis people tend to steer clear of using fixed frequency operators, i.e. not having the pitch of every operator tracking the keyboard. Using one or two fixed frequency operators per sound can create some rather strange abstract effects.

When it comes to abstract synthesis the key is experimentation . . . there are no rules.

Effects ("FX") Synthesis

Effects synthesis is the use of the synthesizer for special non-musical sounds – things like wind, rain, machine guns, space battles, footsteps, men being chased by lawnmowers etc. etc.

In the film and television industry people still use coconuts for horses' hooves, and screw up tissue paper close to the microphone to simulate a crackling fire. Electronics often can't compete with these traditional effects "generators"; initially because they don't sound natural enough, but more specifically because the players don't have the years of skill that the acoustic effects people do. Again, when using the synthesizer for special effects work, you have to be prepared to adopt an unconventional approach to producing the desired sound, and you need to rely heavily on your ears.

ENO:
Originally with Roxy Music, Brian Eno was one of the pioneers of Effects Synthesis. By his own admission his keyboard education was not particularly comprehensive, however he added a totally new dimension to Roxy Music with his remarkable use of a VCS3 synthesizer. Since then his contributions to modern music have been innovative and original, and he has earned himself the acclaim he has amassed over recent years.

The best way to produce a special effect, or an imaginative one, is to get what you think sounds right, then record it on to tape. Also, if possible, program it into one of the memory locations of the instrument you are using. Go away and do something else then return to the sound, play it back on the tape and listen for the faults. Then try and re-create the sound again from scratch, don't recall it from the programmer. This time you will be aware of the sound's shortcomings. You'll find that by using this technique you'll improve the way in which you create particular sounds. If you are working with pictures the battle has been half won before you start. Again, as with imitative synthesis, the brain is lazy, and wants to accept what it is fed. Things have to be pretty out of place for the sounds to be rejected. Say you were putting some sounds to an animation and you were trying to make the sound of a cartoon blackbird bouncing on a telegraph wire. You could get away with virtually any twangy sound. But that sound would not support the scene if you were working for radio. This is by far the most difficult area of effects synthesis.

You will find that Noise is the most useful tool when it comes to effects synthesis, especially when used in conjunction with the filter. It follows, therefore, that analogue instruments are generally more suited to this kind of work, as are modular synthesizers which are incredibly flexible, if somewhat slow to use.

Good synthesis requires musical skill coupled with intuition and technical knowledge of your instrument. Practice and familiarity with your instrument is the key. Moving from a conventional keyboard to a synthesizer is probably one of the biggest steps a musician will make, but don't be in too much of a hurry to keep buying the latest technological wonder. When you have decided on the synthesizer you think suits you best, buy it and stick with it for as long as possible. It takes years to become totally integrated with one particular instrument, to be able to think a sound and to be able to get it.

In addition to all the technical facilities and functions that you want from the instrument, it is important to get a synthesizer to which you can add external control devices and extra voice generators, i.e. make sure it is MIDI equipped (see p. 103), or at the very least can be linked to a MIDI convertor box. Grow with your synthesizer. If you trade it in for a new model, you are throwing away a knowledge and a skill that has taken you maybe several years to perfect.

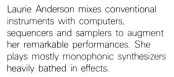

Laurie Anderson mixes conventional instruments with computers, sequencers and samplers to augment her remarkable performances. She plays mostly monophonic synthesizers heavily bathed in effects.

MIDI

12

Virtually all of today's electronic musical instruments utilise a microprocessor (a small computer) as their central brain. Information regarding what notes are being played, what the control knobs say, etc, is fed to the processor which analyses this data and issues instructions to the circuitry that actually makes the sound. A microprocessor is a digital device, and uses binary words or bytes to transmit the information.

Most instruments use bytes of similar format, but they each do so in their own way. It's a bit like Western languages; we use basically the same alphabet as one another, but when the letters are assembled they mean different things in different countries. Now imagine if there were a "black-box" which translated those words into a common language, and which in turn could translate this common tongue back into the host's language (see below). Then everyone could speak to one another. This is exactly what MIDI enables instruments and control devices from any manufacturer to do.

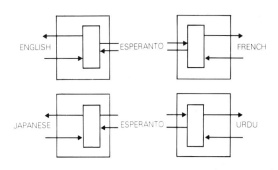

A MIDI equipped instrument has an output and an input socket that puts out and receives a common digital language. The theoretical "black-box" is contained within each instrument (in fact it forms part of the software program that runs the microprocessor). So any two MIDI devices can be connected to one another and data should be able to pass between the two.

MIDI – Why?

MIDI is undoubtedly the most important development of the Eighties in the world of electronic music. But why?

MIDI transmits control information. Let's take the most simple case – controller data. If you play a piece of music on a keyboard, the

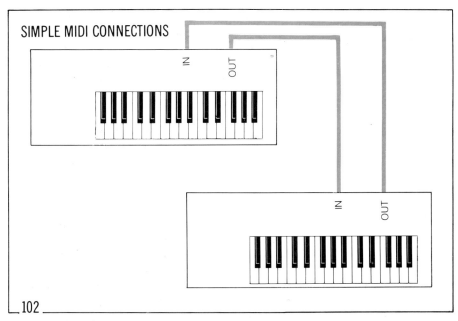

SIMPLE MIDI CONNECTIONS

102

instrument's processor will translate exactly what you are playing into a MIDI encoded signal, this can then be fed to another MIDI'd instrument and exactly the same notes will simultaneously sound on the second instrument. So you're effectively layering two instruments on top of one another, but playing from just one keyboard. This may not appear to be too revolutionary, but the extra sound production possibilities offered by such a system are considerable. For example, with this system you could layer a digital synthesizer and an analogue one, thus establishing a completely new range of composite timbres.

But this is just the tip of the iceberg. Instead of having a second synthesizer, a sequencer could be used to store the MIDI note data, and then it could be played back into the original instrument or sent off to another device whilst a new part was added, etc. But before going any further let's see what kind of information MIDI can actually handle.

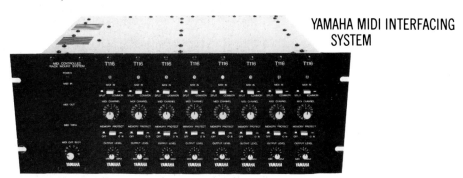

YAMAHA MIDI INTERFACING SYSTEM

Using MIDI

In comparison to the days of the "CV and Gate Ins and Outs" MIDI is an extremely sophisticated language. It can carry, amongst other data, the following information.

1 the notes being played.
2 individual note velocity.
3 key pressure (after touch).
4 program changes.
5 pitch wheel control information.
6 modulation wheel control information.
7 synchronization clock for drum machines/sequencers.
8 voicing information.

But probably the most important aspect of MIDI is that this data can be assigned a particular channel number.

MIDI is designed so that there are sixteen channels. Let's start by considering a simple set-up as shown in figure 102, where two instruments are communicating with one another.

In this example, if 'A' is set to transmit on Channel 1, and 'B' is set to receive on Ch. 1, then anything played on either keyboard will cause both instruments to sound (the MIDI is operating in both directions).

If, however, 'B' was set to Ch. 14 (say), it would be as though no connections existed, neither would respond to the other's signals. In addition to the 16 channels, a MIDI instrument can be set to receive or transmit in "Omni" mode. If 'A' were transmitting on Omni mode, the data would be picked up by 'B' no matter what channel it were set to. Similarly if 'A' was transmitting on Ch. 7 (say), 'B' would only pick up that data if it were either receiving in Omni mode or set to Ch.7.

We've seen that a MIDI equipped instrument has MIDI-in and MIDI-out sockets, but there is a third connection that is important

if you wish to make full use of the MIDI system – MIDI-thru. This simply outputs exactly the same data as is presented to the instrument at the MIDI-in port. The reasons for this will soon become apparent.

It may seem unnecessary to have 16 different MIDI channels, but consider the more complex set-up as shown in figure 103. Here we have a MIDI controller keyboard (a keyboard with no voice modules, but which can output a MIDI signal) connected to a digital sequencer, which in turn is connected to a bank of four MIDI controlled synthesizer voice modules. These are simply synthesizers without keyboards, the controller data coming from the MIDI-input. You will notice that the MIDI connectors run from the output of the sequencer to the MIDI-in of V1, then from the MIDI-thru of V1 to MIDI-in of V2 etc. This enables the output of the sequencer to be fed directly to all voice modules. Note also that V1 is set to MIDI Ch.1, V2 to MIDI Ch.2, etc.

Firstly, the controller is set to MIDI Ch.1 and a passage of notes played. These notes will be stored in the sequencer as being assigned to Ch.1, and on replay they will trigger only V1. The controller can then be set to Ch.2 and a passage of notes overdubbed on to the first line. This will activate only V2. So in this way it is possible to build up a multi-channel recording assigning different parts to different voice modules by giving each a separate channel number. You can now see why it is useful to have 16 different channels; it's like having a 16 track tape recorder. Some people, however, complain that 16 is not enough.

The Hardware

CONNECTORS: The 3 sockets to be found on the back of most MIDI instruments are of the 5-pin DIN (180 degree) variety. These are similar to the plugs found on many hi-fi amps

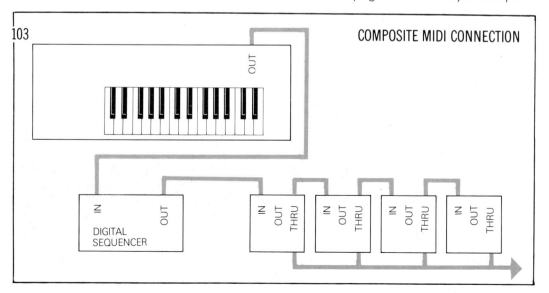

103   COMPOSITE MIDI CONNECTION

for the Record/Playback connection to a tape recorder, but obviously such a connection should not be made. Unfortunately Roland and Korg instruments also utilise the same connector for their "Sync" data. Again a MIDI port or socket should not be connected to a Sync outlet.

CABLE: As you can see from figure 104 only pins 2, 4, and 5 are used. The best cable to use is a shielded twisted pair.
   This cable consists of two wires twisted together with a third conductor wrapped around the pair to shield them. The cable should not be more than 15 meters in length, otherwise problems will occur.

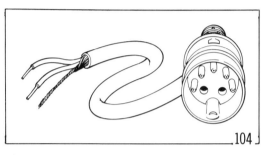
104

The following information is for the more technically orientated reader. It is not necessary to understand the physical 'construction' of the MIDI interface.

INTERFACE: The actual circuitry used to translate the digital signal into the signal that travels down the MIDI cable is shown in figure\104. The use of optoisolators ensures that incorrect connection to the MIDI port does not damage the control circuitry of the instrument. This circuit operates using a 1.5mA current loop, with Logical 0 turning the current ON. Rise and Fall times need to be less than 2 microseconds.

SPECIFICATIONS: The MIDI interface runs asynchronously at 31.25 (+/- 1%) kbauds. The interface is a serial one with each byte consisting of a start bit, 8 data bits (Do to D7) then a stop bit, making 10 bits. Thus each byte occupies 320 microseconds.

MIDI Messages
The transmission of MIDI information is relatively simple. Any MIDI event (e.g. the playing of a note) causes a message to be sent down the line and the receiving instrument or device acts accordingly.
   Most MIDI "messages" consist of a status byte, and one or two data bytes. That is to say, the message consists of two words. The first says "the next piece of information you are going to receive relates to the pitch bend control (say)", and the second word says "the

All of these instruments are MIDI standard, and as such can be connected together and programmed collectively.

pitch bend control has moved up a semitone (or whatever)". So the receiving instrument knows what to do with the data.

MIDI messages fall into two main categories:

1 Channel Messages. These contain a channel number encoded in their status byte; so unless the receiving device is set to that channel it will ignore the message. The most common type of channel message relates to note on and note off information.

2 System Messages. These go to all devices that are MIDI'd up, i.e. they contain no channel number. There are three types of message:

● System Real Time – messages that send Timing signals, Clock Start, Stop, and Continue commands, etc. System Real commands consist of Status Bytes only – no Data bytes.

● System Common – commands for all devices. These include such signals as: Song Select, which specifies which song or sequence is to be played upon receipt of a Start message; and Song Pointer transmits where you are in the song or sequence.

● System Exclusive – this message is used to send specific information to instruments made by specific manufacturers. For example, the Sequential Sequencer 64 and 910 software can be used to program the Sequential Sixtrak synthesizer. The software is such that no other MIDI instrument will be 'interested', so the data is preceded by a Systems exclusive command which says that

the following data is applicable only to a certain manufacturer's instrument. There follows a data byte which specifies the company in question, and then the data bytes with the relevant information are transmitted. A final "End of Systems Exclusive" byte is required to say that all the data has been transmitted. (see figure 105).

Running Status

The most critical elements transmitted via the MIDI link are note on and off data. Because the system is a serial one, note information has to be stacked up one event after another. So if a 10 note chord were to be played then each of these would require two binary words each lasting 320 microseconds to signify just the "Note Ons". That takes 6.4 milliseconds, which is pretty slow. If, in addition, key velocity and other data has also to be transmitted, the time delay gets even longer.

To try and speed things up a facility known as Running Status is used. This applies only to channel messages. When a train of similar messages all with the same Status byte (like Note On) is being transmitted, the status bytes are omitted. The messages then consist of one status byte at the beginning followed by a stream of different data bytes. Only when some other form of message has to be sent does a new Status byte appear. Real Time messages will, of course, interrupt things, as is their way.

Running Status does make things a lot faster, but the system is being pushed to its limit, and already demands are being made to introduce some new form of Super-MIDI spec. The problem with such a requirement is that it has to be compatible with the present interface.

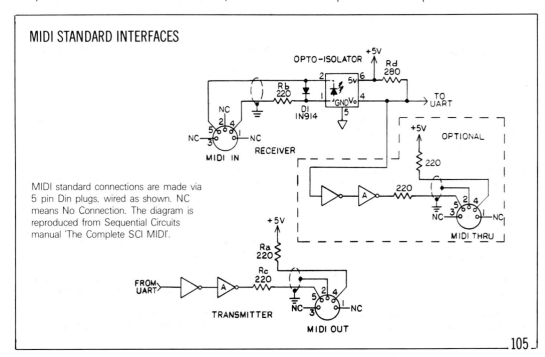

MIDI STANDARD INTERFACES

MIDI standard connections are made via 5 pin Din plugs, wired as shown. NC means No Connection. The diagram is reproduced from Sequential Circuits manual 'The Complete SCI MIDI'.

GLOSSARY

A

Additive Synthesis: The construction of more complex tones from a series of fundamental frequencies (i.e. sine waves). This synthesis technique relies on the principle that any periodic waveshape can be constructed by adding together sine waves of varying amplitudes and frequencies.

Address: a location in a memory bank where a certain piece of data is stored.

ADSR: An abbreviation of Attack, Decay, Sustain, Release — the four prime parameters to be found as part of an envelope generator.

Algorithm: The way in which several operators are arranged with respect to one another. Some operators will act as modifiers others as carriers. (an FM Synthesis term)

Amplitude: The amount of any signal is known as its amplitude. In respect of an audio signal, the amplitude corresponds to the loudness at which we perceive the signal. In electrical terms, the amplitude is a measurement of the amount a voltage is fluctuating.

Amplitude Modulation: In a synthesizer, the amplitude of a signal can be controlled by a voltage. If this voltage is changing, then the signal is said to be experiencing amplitude modulation. The most common form of modulation is tremolo, which occurs when a sub-audio oscillation, usually in the form of a sine wave, is used to modulate the amplitude.

Analogue: A signal or voltage that is continuously variable, i.e. one that can theoretically be set at any level. An analogue device is one that responds directly to a control voltage.

Analogue/Digital Convertor: A device that will sample an analogue signal (voltage) and transform it into a digital representation of that signal. This digital code can then be subsequently processed by other digital devices.

Analogue Sequencer: A sequencer that handles continuous analogue signals. Normally, this device generates its own control signals, providing a series of control voltages and gate/trigger pulses that are set up manually on the control panel. These voltages are fed out in series to the synthesizer.

Aperiodic Waveform: An irregular, non-repeating waveform without pitch.

Assignment: A term that is applicable to polyphonic synthesizers, referring to the determination as to which voice module is to be controlled by which note currently being played.

Attack: A parameter of the envelope generator. This is the time, at the start of the envelope, that the output voltage takes to reach its peak level.

Attenuator: A device that is used to reduce the amplitude of the signal passing through it.

Azure Noise: A random signal, weighted so that the higher frequencies are more pronounced. Can be heard as a hissing sound.

B

Balanced Modulator: See **Ring Modulator.**

Band Pass Filter: A device that allows only those signals around a certain frequency (the cut-off frequency) to pass.

Band Reject (Notch) Filter: A device designed to allow all frequencies, other than those around a certain frequency (the cut-off frequency) to pass.

Beat: The interaction caused by two closely related pitches sounding simultaneously. This interaction takes the form of a wavering in the loudness of the total sound, and is a useful means of tuning two pitches together (eliminating the beats).

Bit: Part of a byte (a digital word) — a single binary digit which can either be '1' or '0'.

Break Point: The place at which the keyboard is split.

C

Carrier: A term used in FM Synthesis which is applied to an operator that is actually heard rather than one that is used to modulate.

Cartridge Memory: A plug in package that is used to store data — usually voicing information. A cartridge will generally house some form of random access memory.

Centre Dente: A physical notch in a control mechanism (potentiometer, slider, etc.) that enables the operator to return the control to its original centre position after use. Particularly common on pitch-bend controls.

Chip: Silicon Chip. A small sliver of silicon upon which is etched an electronic circuit, thus allowing vast amounts of circuitry to be contained within a device no larger than a coin.

Clamping: The limitation of a voltage to a specified level.

Clock: Regular low frequency pulse waveform used for driving sequencers, control sampling, time storage of information, triggering etc.

Computer Interface: A device that allows a computer to talk to another device.

Contour: See **Envelope**

Contour Amount: Control that determines the amount of effect the envelope generator will have over the voltage controlled parameter it is driving (normally the VCF or VCA).

Control Voltage: A signal that is used to tell voltage controllable parameters what to do.

Cosine Wave: A waveform of identical shape to a sine wave, but 90 degrees (¼ of a cycle) out of phase with it.

Cut-Off Frequency: The frequency at which the filter is set to operate. This parameter is normally both voltage controllable and manually variable.

D

DCO: Digitally Controlled Oscillator — a device generating an output signal whose pitch is determined by the digital control signal applied to it.

Decay: A parameter of the envelope generator, it is the rate at which the output voltage falls from its maximum level before reaching the sustain level. For ADR, the decay setting also determines the time that the output voltage takes to die away to zero after the key has been released.

Decibel: The most common unit for measuring the loudness of sound. The decibel is a ratio of two numbers, one being a reference level. Audible sounds range from 0 dB, the threshold of hearing, to 120 dB, the threshold of pain.

Default: The settings that a device opts for when it is initially switched on.

Delay: A term normally associated with the LFO, where it refers to the time taken for the LFO to start to modulate a voltage controllable parameter after the note has been pressed — hence, delayed vibrato when used in conjunction with VCOs. Delay is also a parameter of the five stage envelope generator (DADSR), where it varies the time between the triggering of the envelope generator, and the time when the envelope voltage starts to rise (the attack).

Digital: The representation of a signal by a binary number. Digital equipment manipulates these binary numbers as opposed to the analogue use of continuously variable signals. A digital signal (not be be confused with a quantized one) consists of a train of pulses that have only two states — high or low.

Digital/Analogue Converter: A device that will generate an analogue voltage corresponding to the digital signal applied to it.

Digital Sequencer: A device that will store a series of events in the form of a digital code in an integrated memory device. The sequence, on recall, is fed through a digital/analogue converter to provide a control voltage for driving a synthesizer. A digital sequencer is normally programmed by playing the desired pattern of notes on the keyboard, whence control signals are fed into the sequencer and converted into the digital information.

Direct Synthesis: A series of numbers representing the instantaneous values of voltage levels at different points in a waveform are stored in a computer memory, and called forth as necessary to produce the desired sound.

Drift: The unintentional variation of a certain voice module parameter, e.g. the pitch of the oscillator might slowly drift out of tune.

Droop: As with drift, this is an unwanted variation in a control voltage. For example, in earlier instruments, the keyboard voltage memory, which remembered what note had been played last, was prone to leakage, and the voltage would tend to decrease slowly — this is known as droop.

Duophonic: The capacity of a synthesizer to play two notes simultaneously. Normally, this necessitates the use of two separate synthesizer voice modules; however, some instruments provide a pseudo-duophonic feature, by assigning separate oscillators to each note and sharing all the other parameters (VCF's, VCA's etc.).

Duty Cycle: The proportion of time a rectangular wave spends in a "high" state compared to the time as a "low". Normally, this is expressed as a percentage, so a square wave would have a 50 per cent duty cycle.

Dynamic Range: With respect to the synthesizer, this term applies to the range of control that a touch responsive keyboard will provide.

Dynamics: The dynamics of a sound are the changes that take place over its duration. These changes are generally with respect to timbre and amplitude.

E

Echo: A repetition of a sound that is distinct from the original. A series of echoes are normally accompanied by a decrease in amplitude. If the amplitude increases, then there will be a feedback problem.

Edit: To change certain parameters of a sound, or to change part of a sequence.

EEPROM: Electronically Erasable Programmable Read Only Memory. A memory device that will store information even when the power is turned off. However, the information can be erased by applying a particular kind of signal. An EEPROM equates to a hybrid RAM.

Emphasis: See **Resonance.**

Envelope: A voltage that changes as a function of time. It is generally triggered by the controller, and used to shape the amplitude and timbre of a note.

EPROM: Erasable Programmable Read Only Memory. A small electronic component (chip) used by manufacturers to store data that will not need to be continually changed — i.e. a set of program instructions. This information can only be erased by bathing the chip in ultra violet light.

Equal (Even) Temperament: A scaling system whereby the octave is divided into twelve equal parts. The frequency ratio between any two adjacent notes (semitones) is exactly the same. This system is employed by all synthesizer manufacturers as it is a far simpler system to design, and use.

Equalizer: A device used to enhance, or attenuate, certain fixed frequency bands of a signal. It can be considered as a complex, but static, tone control system.

Event: A distinct musical occurrence, with pitch, timbre, loudness and duration all defined.

Exponential: A relationship between two values such that a change in one causes a non-linear response to the other. For example, the "one volt per octave" is an exponential relationship — the frequency is doubling for every one volt increase. A "one volt per 1000 Hz", however, is a linear relationship.

F

Feedback: A path from a device's output back to the input. The term is often used to explain the resonance control of the filter, where some of the output is fed back to the input to accentuate the frequencies around the cut-off point.

Filter: A device used to remove, or block, certain frequencies from an audio or sub-audio signal. The voltage controlled filter found in most synthesizer voice modules is also capable of emphasizing the frequencies around the cut-off point. (See **Band Pass, Band Reject, High Pass** and **Low Pass Filters**).

F.M. Synthesis: Frequency Modulation Synthesis. A method of creating sounds by means of the controlled frequency modulation of sine waves.

Force Sensitivity: See **Pressure Sensitivity**

Frequency Modulation: The frequency of a voltage controlled oscillator, or filter, can be varied by applying a control voltage to it. Thus, if the voltage is changing, then the circuit is being frequency modulated. Vibrato is the most common form of frequency modulation, occurring when a sub-audio sine wave is used to modulate the frequency of a VCO.

Fundamental: When analysing a waveshape, the fundamental is the lowest frequency element present. It is generally the strongest, in terms of amplitude, and it is this frequency that gives the sound its overall musical pitch.

G

Gain: The factor by which a device increases the amplitude of an audio, or sub-audio signal. A negative gain factor results in the attenuation of the signal.

Gate: A control signal generated by the controller (keyboard), which indicates whether a key is being pressed or not. A gate signal will be present until the time that no key is being played. Therefore, it indicates to the synthesizer voice module the start, duration, and end of a note.

Glide: The slewing of a voltage between two levels. The result is a smooth change in pitch between the two notes played.

Glissando: The automatic stepping in semitones between notes. The effect is equivalent to playing every note between the two notes actually triggered.

Glitch: A fault in a system which causes it to operate in an unsatisfactory manner. Used to describe a non-perfect computer programme, and a poorly set looped section of a sample.

Growl: Low frequency sine wave modulation of the filter cut-off frequency.

H

Hard-wired: Electrical routing of signals that is incorporated into the instrument's design. The routing may in some cases be overridden, but usually they follow the standard "controller – VCO – VCF – VCA" configuration.

Harmonics: The various frequency components present in complex sounds. All harmonics are simple multiples of the fundamental frequency.

Hertz (Hz)**:** Measurements of frequency. One Hertz (1 Hz) corresponds to one vibration every second.

High Note Priority: A monophonic synthesizer will play only one note at a time. If more than one is pressed at any instant in time, a high note priority system will assign the top note to the synthesizer voice module.

High Pass Filter: A device that allows only those signals above the cut-off point to pass.

Hybrid: A respected design group based in Covent Garden.

I

Interface: Two devices are said to be interfaced when arranged such that one is controlling the other – e.g. interfacing a synthesizer and sequencer.

Inverter: A circuit that turns a signal upside down, so that positive going signals become negative going. A ramp up sawtooth wave will become a ramp down.

J

Joystick: A control mechanism that is normally used as a performance control. It consists of a lever that can move both up and down as well as left and right (some joysticks will rotate as well). The advantage of the joystick is that several functions can be controlled with one mechanism.

Just Intonation: A scaling system whereby the octave is divided into twelve unequal divisions. The scale of just intonation produces harmony which is pleasing to the ear because of the closely related, though not equal , interval relations. However, this system causes major tuning problems when accompanying instruments using fixed tuning systems – equal temperament.

K

Keyboard Priority: Various systems are employed to assign the voice module to the notes played on the keyboard. The priority modes sort out which note is to sound when more than one is activated on a monophonic instrument. See **High**, **Low** and **Last Note Priority**.

L

Lag: An effect that smooths out rapid changes in voltage. This is obtained by using a very low frequency low pass filter.

Last Note Priority: When more than one note is played simultaneously, this system will cause the last one played to sound.

Latching: A procedure that memorizes a certain parameter, e.g. the interval between two oscillators.

Layering: The use of more than one voice module per note, in order to build up a composite voicing.

LFO: The low frequency oscillator, which operates in the sub-audio frequencies producing a wide range of different waveforms that are used for modulation purposes.

Linear: A linear relationship between two values is such that a change in one causes a proportional change in the other. See **Exponential**.

Loop: A term used in sampling to specify a sustained part of the sample. If a note is held this portion of the sample will continue to repeat itself until the key is released.

Low Note Priority: If two or more notes are simultaneously played, then, when using this system, the lowest one being held will sound.

Low-Pass Filter: A filter designed to allow all frequencies below the cut-off point to pass.

M

Merge: A combination of sequences.

MIDI: Musical Instrument Digital Interface. The "universal" language that enables digital devices to communicate with one another.

Modifier: A device that acts on an audio signal so that, in some way, it changes its character.

Modular: A modular synthesizer can be considered as a collection of discrete building blocks – VCO's, VCF's, VCA's, envelope generators, etc. – which are hooked up together by patch leads or some similar medium, in a configuration to produce the desired effect. Each block can be considered as a module, and can be replaced if necessary with a different device. Most modular systems aren't hard-wired, so any unconventional signal flow can be accommodated.

Modulation: The application of a periodic, or aperiodic control voltage to a voltage controllable parameter in order to change the character of the audio signal.

Modulation Index: The ratio between the output level of a modulator operator and the level of the carrier it is modulating – an FM synthesis term.

Module: A device that makes up part of a modular system. See also **Voice Module**.

Monochord: An effect possible on a monophonic, multi-oscillator synthesizer. The oscillators are tuned to certain intervals, (e.g. the fundamental, third and fifth), and this fixed chord is transposed by the keyboard's (controller) control voltage.

Multiple: Found only on modular systems, this passive circuit enables a signal or control voltage to be split and sent off to two or more other modules.

Multiple Trigger: A triggering system employed by certain manufacturers whereby a new trigger pulse is generated every time a new key is struck, even if previously held keys haven't been released.

N

Negative Feedback: Occurring when part of the signal from the output of a device (e.g. an amplifier or filter) is fed back to the input, but with its polarity or phase opposite to that of the input signal. This leads to a dampening of the resulting signal.

Noise Generator: A source of random voltage fluctuations, which, when converted to an audible signal, sound like a radio that is tuned in between VHF channels.

Non-Volatile Memory: A type of memory system, that will retain the information it possesses even when the power has been switched off.

Notch Filter: See **Band Reject Filter**.

O

One Shot: An event that has to be re-triggered every time it is required to occur, i.e. a single event.

Operator: A term used in FM Synthesis to describe a circuit element consisting of a digitally controlled sine wave generator, a digitally controlled envelope generator and an amplifier.

Oscillator: An electronic circuit that produces a constantly repeating waveform.

Overtones: The various frequency components that make up a sound. These may be of any mathematical relationship to the fundamental. See also **Harmonics**.

P

Parameter: Any part of a sound that can be varied to change the character of the sound, e.g. attack time, cut-off frequency, modulation index etc.

Patch: The way in which the various synthesizer blocks are hooked up. See **Hard-wired**.

Patch Cords/Leads: The cables that are used to hook up the various sections of a modular system.

Performance Controls: The group of controls situated close to the keyboard (controller) that are used to modify the character of the note whilst it is sounding. Normally, these control some form of pitchbender, a modulation control, a master volume, and a portamento rate control.

Periodic: A regular repeating waveform, thus exhibiting pitch.

Phase: The point in the cycle of a periodic waveform where the oscillator is, at any particular instance. Two sine waves, for example, may be of the same frequency and sound the same, but, if they started their cycles at different times, they would have a different phase relationship. The period the two waves are apart is known as the phase difference or phase angle.

Phase Distortion Synthesis: A form of synthesis that utilises mathematically distorted sine waves as the basic sound source. The sine wave can be violently distorted to form virtually any other waveform.

Phase Locking: A circuit that detects the difference in phase between two signals and then changes the frequency of one so that they match.

Pink Noise: A random combination of all frequencies in equal amounts over each octave of the audio spectrum.

Pitch bend: See **Bend**.

Pitch to Voltage Converter: A device that measures the frequency of an incoming signal and produces a control voltage proportional to this frequency, such that, when the voltage is applied to a VCO, the pitch of the oscillator will track that of the incoming signal.

Port: An access point, usually on the rear panel of an instrument, that allows the user to tap into the signal chain.

Portamento: See **Glide**.

Positive Feedback: This occurs when the signal that is fed back to the device from the output has the same polarity or phase as the input. The feedback signal, therefore, tends to reinforce the input signal – often to such a degree that self-oscillation occurs.

Pre-patched: See **Hard-wired**.

Preset: A button or switch used to select a certain preprogrammed voicing. When selected, all the variable parameters of the synthesizer voice module are automatically set to produce the desired sound.

Pressure Sensitivity: A feature of certain keyboards sometimes known as second touch. It refers to the generation of an additional control voltage, the level of which is dependent on how much pressure is applied to the key after it has been depressed. This voltage can be used to bend the pitch, open the filter, increase the amplitude, etc.

Programmable: The ability to store a certain patch in a memory circuit so that the sound can be recalled and recreated at a later time.

Pulse Wave: A waveshape generated by an oscillator consisting of an alternating high and low steady state voltage.

Pulse Width: See **Duty Cycle**.

Pulse Width Modulation: The automatic variation in the pulse width or duty cycle of a pulse wave by a control signal (normally, the LFO). The resulting effect is the fattening up of the sound – comparable with the sound of two oscillators almost in unison.

Q

Q: See **Resonance**.

Quantized: A continuously changing voltage is quantized by slotting it into specific voltage steps, i.e. the voltage can exist only as certain values. The most common form of quantizing is that of converting the voltages produced by potentiometers (control knobs) such that, when it is applied to a voltage controlled oscillator, the pitch will sweep in semitonal steps.

Quick Disc: A new form of fast memory storage rather like a floppy disc, but read sequentially rather than in a random access manner.

R

Ramp Wave: An oscillator output waveform that rises smoothly to a peak, then drops instantaneously to its starting point. This waveform can be either of two states; ramp up, as described above; or ramp down, the above inverted. The ramp wave has a brassy quality to it due to its relatively rich harmonic content.

Random Access: The ability to access specific data directly. An audio disc is a good illustration of this principle – you can get to any part of the recording virtually instantaneously by moving the arm to the desired section (random access), whereas an audio cassette has to be spooled from the start before getting to the desired section (sequential).

Release: The envelope generator parameter that governs how long it takes for the output voltage to return to its initial position after the key (hence gate) has been released.

Resonance: This is caused by applying positive feedback around the filter, and has the effect of causing those frequencies close to the cut-off point to be emphasized to an extent that a ringing can be detected. Extreme degrees of resonance result in the filter breaking into self-oscillation.

Ribbon: A controller that puts out a voltage dependent on where along its surface it is pressed. It is most commonly used for pitchbending.

Ringing: See **Resonance**.

Ring Modulator: A device that accepts two audio signals and puts out two different signals, one consisting of the arithmetic sum of the input frequencies, the other the difference. This circuit is most often used in the production of a clangorous sound, e.g. bells and gongs etc.

Roll-off: The rate at which a signal is attenuated by a filter. Ideally, all frequencies beyond the cut-off point of a filter would be removed completely; however, this isn't the case, and the roll-off characteristic of a filter identifies the rate of attenuation of these filtered signals. The roll-off is measured in dB/octave.

S

Sample and Hold: A device that accepts a clock pulse, and samples a given signal on every pulse from the clock. The voltage at this instant is held in the circuit's memory until the next clock pulse samples a new level.

Sampling: A form of synthesis based on an existing sound. A sound is digitally encoded in the memory of the instrument and this data is manipulated so as to provide the sound at different pitches across the span of the keyboard or controller. A wide range of further signal processing is generally available to make greater use of the sample.

Sawtooth Wave: See **Ramp Wave**.

Scaling: A normal controller will double the frequency of the oscillators for every octave jump. However, some synthesizers have a variable scaling facility enabling a microtonal scaling to be set up.

Schmitt Tiger: A device that samples an incoming signal, and puts out a pulse every time that signal goes over a predetermined threshold level.

Self-Oscillation: See **Resonance**.

Sequential Memory: See **Random Access**.

Sine Wave: A smooth, continuously changing waveform that has a pure tone. It is a fundamental waveform with no overtones or harmonics.

Single Trigger: This is a system employed on certain instruments whereby a new trigger pulse is generated only when all the other keys have been released. This enables the playing of legato passages without retriggering the envelope generators.

Square Wave: A pulse wave with a 50 per cent duty cycle. It has a clear, hollow quality to it.

Static Filter: A filter whose characteristics remain fixed once set by the front panel controls, i.e. it isn't voltage controllable.

Step Time: The division of note lengths into equal units of time. Thus to program a complex sequence, one step must equate to the lowest common denominator – a sixteenth note maybe.

Subtractive Synthesis: A system of synthesis whereby the starting point is a waveform rich in harmonics, which is then processed by a series of harmonic filters in order to remove unwanted harmonics and so produce the desired sound.

Sustain: The third phase of the ADSR envelope, this is the level at which the envelope output settles down for as long as the key remains held.

Switch Trigger: A type of trigger signal that produces a shorting to ground at the outputs when activated. It is, therefore, a simple process to parallel up various such trigger sources.

Synchronization: The locking together of two oscillators at the beginning of one of their cycles.

T

Timbre: The tonal quality of a sound that distinguishes notes of the same pitch and amplitude.

Touch Pad/Switch: A control that has no moving parts, but is activated merely by touch. It can be used to switch any parameter that is controlled by a mechanical switch.

Touch Responsive: A control that has no moving parts, but is activated merely by touch. It can be used to switch any parameter that is controlled by a mechanical switch.

Touch Sensitive: Applies to a type of keyboard that can sense the speed or pressure with which a key is struck and produce a proportional control voltage.

Transient Generator: See **Envelope.**

Tremolo: See **Amplitude Modulation.**

Triangle Wave: An oscillator output waveform that rises smoothly to a peak, then falls at a similar rate until it reaches its starting point whence it repeats. It has a smooth, muted tonal quality, a bit like a sine wave, though because of its harmonic content it is less pure.

Trigger: A signal produced by the controller that tells the envelope generators when to start their cycles.

U

Unison: When two or more oscillators are running at the same frequency.

V

Variable: A control parameter that is continuously variable, i.e. one that isn't just on or off, nor, strictly speaking, quantized.

VCA: Voltage Controlled Amplifier. A device that adjusts the volume of a signal proportionally to the control voltage applied to it.

VCF: Voltage Controlled Filter: A filter whose cut-off frequency is proportional to the voltage applied to it. Some VCFs also provide voltage controllable resonance.

VCO: Voltage Controlled Oscillator: A device generating an output signal of frequency proportional to the voltage applied to it.

Vernier: A scale (measuring device) fixed to potentiometer in place of a knob, which enables that parameter to be set at a particular position with a high degree of accuracy.

Vibrato: See **Frequency Modulation.**

Vocoder: A device that analyses the frequency content of an incoming signal, and uses that information to control a bank of filters that are to process a second signal. In this way, a sound can retain its original pitch yet take on the timbral characteristics of another sound. Alternatively, inanimate sounds can be pitched into a chromatic scale.

Voice Module: The combined forces of oscillators, filter, amplifier, envelope generators, low frequency oscillators, all the blocks that are used to make a synthesized sound can be considered as a whole — a voice module.

Volatile Memory: A memory system that requires a constant power source in order to retain the information in it. If the power fails, the information is permanently lost.

Voltage Control: The basis of operation for most synthesizers. Voltages are used to change parameters as desired. The advantage of this system is that most circuits produce voltages, so one device can be used to control another, and so on.

Voltage Trigger: A type of triggering signal that consists of a fast change in voltage — either positive or negative.

W

Waveform Modulation: A voltage controlled change in the shape of a given waveform, without any corresponding change in frequency.

Wheel: A form of performance control, normally used for pitchbending or modulation.

White Noise: A random combination of all frequencies in equal amounts over the entire audio spectrum.

ACKNOWLEDGEMENTS

The illustrations for this book were by:
Brian Sayers: all airbrush art and line drawings of musical instruments.
Kevin Jones: System diagrams
Liz Dixon: Line diagrams

Grateful thanks to: Akai, Casio, Chromatix, EMU, Ensoniq Pacifex, Lexicon, Moog, Oberheim, The Oxford Synthesizer Co., Roland UK, Rose Morris for Korg, Sequential Circuits, Synthaxe, Turnkey, The Welsh Tourist Board, Yamaha.
Also the following record companies:
Island, Parlophone, Polydor, RCA, Virgin, Warner Bros.

Special thanks to Debbie Rhodes, Julia Harris, Chris Mehan, Perry Neville, Claudia Zeff, Jon Nel and Martha Ellen Zenfell, without whose help this book would not have been possible.